WATFORD TO WOO

CH00862842

Born in São Paulo in 1953 an
Moxley left school at 16, joined the
around the world as a seaman, bo.
numerous other jobs before entering the world of finance. His
travels took him to Africa, Alaska, Asia, Australia, Oceania,
North and South America. This is his first book and the story of
his adventures. He lives in Devon with his Australian cattle dogs,
Breaker and Bundy.

WATFORD

TO

WOOLLOOMOOLOO

John Moxley

Cover photos from "Life's a Beach" collection, Jill Grayson

Watford to Woolloomooloo

ISBN: 978-1-4716-4903-5

First edition 2012
Second edition 2013
Third edition 2014
Revised 2014

Acknowledgements

Thanks and acknowledgements to the publishers and copyright holders for permission to reproduce quotations from the following works:

The Rubaiyat of Omar Khayyam translated by Edward FitzGerald, illustrated by Marjorie Anderson, foreword by Laurence Housman. London: Collins Clear Type Press.

Sea fever: Selected poems of John Masefield edited by Philip Errington. Manchester: Fyfield Books, 2005. Thanks to The Society of Authors as the Literary Representative of the Estate of John Masefield.

How to talk dirty and influence people by Lenny Bruce. New York: Fireside, 1992.

Striking thoughts: Bruce Lee's wisdom for daily living by Bruce Lee and John Little. Vermont: Tuttle Publishing, 2002.

Miyamoto Musashi: His life and writings by Kenji Tokitsu (translated by Sherab Chodzin Kohn). London: Weatherhill, 2005.

Thanks for permission to use digital images to The Florida Times-Union, Kees Helder (Helderline), Bruce Strong, Rob & Stephanie Levy, Jack Moxley, Julian@Soul Aperture, James Penman, Richard & Vicki, John Law, Mark Wheaver, Robert Opie collection@Museum of Brands, Ian & Dianna Dent, Jim Shelley, Paul Wright, Pepijn van Erp, Steve Waite, Barney Boylan, Boodarai, Jimmy Still, Dennis Hopkins.

I would like to acknowledge Lynne and Elaine of Jahanghir Kennels for encouraging me to write this book in the first place, Ken Moxley for invaluable research of family history, and Hilton Grayson for reading, editing and invaluable advice regarding the manuscript and assistance with electronic files and images, and without whose support it would never have been finished.

I would also like to express my gratitude to Jill Grayson who kindly checked and provided suggestions for my book and who generously allowed me to use her photos for the covers.

Cover art by T. Hilton Grayson.

Contents

J23. Plymouth School of Navigation, 1970 (courtesy of Jimmy Still).

One thing is certain, that life flies; one thing is certain, and the rest is lies; the flower that once has blown for ever dies. Omar Khayyam

1
From humble beginnings

The solicitor's office was bright and tidy and I was not expecting much more than a brief instruction on how to present myself in the best possible light when I went up before the magistrate. It was only when he mentioned the possibility of a custodial sentence, something I had not even considered for what I perceived to be a relatively minor indiscretion, that I realised maybe this time I had overstepped the mark. In retrospect, it should have come as no surprise; over a period of many years I had rebelled against authority and the position I now found myself in was the inevitable result. My school record left much to be desired and the threat of expulsion was still fresh in my mind after an incident which left another lad needing medical attention; I think it was only the fact that he had called me a 'wog' that saved me, although the race card carried little weight in those days so I could not be sure. Surprisingly, my academic performance was more than passable, considering the total lack of commitment or effort I invested in it.

This was all a far cry from São Paulo, Brasil, where I was born and spent the first five years of my life, but, according to my parents, that was where my propensity for trouble started. My father worked as an accountant for Vestey Brothers. His own father had died leaving his widow with six boys and pregnant with my father, and to say times were hard as they grew up in North London would be an understatement. They struggled through and at the outbreak of war all seven brothers joined up to do their bit. My father was a navigator in the RAF, and after the war he went to night school to qualify as an accountant. His quiet, unassuming demeanour masked a fierce determination and he was not easily intimidated. His first posting was Brasil.

The story my parents told was how, as a four year old, I would run home crying because the big boy over the road had hit me, again. No doubt embarrassed at this pathetic show of cowardice, my father insisted on showing me how to punch back. I soon had reason to put the theory to the test and it proved to be a resounding success, with the big boy running home in tears instead of me. I could clearly see the potential of this approach and must have instinctively adopted it as a means of resolving a threat or confrontation. This had not been my father's intention, of course, but it was too late: the genie was out of the bottle.

When we returned to the UK we finally settled in Watford, a town about as close as you could get to London without being swallowed up by it. The town centre was, basically, just one long road, the High Street, and everything of note was on it. The close proximity to London meant that it was always at the forefront of whatever was new on the scene, whether that was fashion, music or drugs. If they didn't have it in the High Street then a twenty minute train ride from Watford Junction took you to the heart of the West End, and there you could get anything and everything. It was like having the best of both worlds: access to the bright lights whenever you wanted but the laid back atmosphere of a small town for day to day living. It would have been easy to support Arsenal, Chelsea, or Tottenham but we didn't, it had to be Watford, or 'the Hornets' as they were affectionately known; we were proud to come from Watford.

It is my experience that most people who grow up in big cities tend to be one step ahead of the rest, the pace of life just makes you that much quicker off the mark and when it came to big cities, London was 'the Daddy' in the 60's. There was no competition and we were led to believe that everybody west of Reading was a country bumpkin and civilisation stopped just north of Watford.

But the times were changing, as Bob Dylan was observant

enough to point out, and the days of Mods and Rockers fighting it out on Brighton seafront every Bank holiday were drawing to a close. There were some new kids on the block: Hippies and Skinheads. The Hippies were against violence of any kind, the war in Vietnam was a focal issue for them; they dressed in flowery kaftans, smoked pot, wore flowers in their hair and preached peace and free love. They grew their hair long and got stoned at parties to Jimi Hendrix, Tyrannosaurus Rex and John Mayall's Bluesbreakers. The Skinheads wore rolled up Levis, red braces and Doc Marten boots, liked a bit of 'bovver', danced to reggae, soul and ska, and took Dexies (uppers) and Mandies (downers) as the need arose. As I had now reached the grand old age of fifteen I had to decide which tribe I was going to join and, as there was no way I was going to walk around in a flowery kaftan, the decision wasn't really difficult.

There are many misconceptions about Skinheads, they were portrayed as racist thugs but their whole ethos was built around black music like ska and soul, and it was the Skinheads who, without question, championed reggae music from its raw beginnings through to the melodies of Bob Marley. I never saw so much as a scuffle between a Skinhead and a Black, their aggression was, for the most part, directed at Skinhead gangs from other towns. As is usually the case, the violence was nowhere near as bad as reported; it's true there were running battles with other groups of football supporters as they arrived at Watford Junction, but the heavy police presence usually meant that there was more verbal posturing than actual fisticuffs. I am not trying to rewrite history and would be lying if I said that the Skinheads didn't cause their share of trouble, but the real villains of the piece were the numbskulls who came along well over a decade later and adopted the shaved head, along with the swastika tattoo and the flag of St George, as emblems of their neo-Nazi doctrine. They were a totally different breed altogether and were easily spotted by their inability to string more than two words together.

Anyway, as mere lads of sixteen we would just hang around

the High Street of an evening wasting time and seeing what mischief we could get up to, no different to teenagers of any generation, really. It was not difficult to see where this was leading and, in my defence, I had seen the writing on the wall a few months previously and tried to join the Royal Marines. I saw it as the ideal ticket out of my wayward life but, as is often the way, it wasn't that straightforward. It meant signing on for nine years with no option to buy myself out, and while I did not see this as a problem, I needed my parents' signature and they were not prepared, as they saw it, to sign away my life. The recruitment sergeant came round to the house one evening in an attempt to convince my father and although his tales of action and adventure fired my imagination it failed to change my father's mind.

I always felt sorry for my parents; they were hard working newsagents, up at five every morning to mark up the newspapers for delivery and worked seven days a week. They were God-fearing and highly principled with a daughter who was the pride and joy of the local Grammar school and whose future in academia was assured. I was the black sheep of the family.

The incident that landed me in the solicitor's office was nothing to shout about; me and a couple of friends had been hanging around town having a few laughs before making our way home. As we strolled through the grounds of the local Polytechnic, probably a university by now, we saw a scooter parked in a quiet corner. We went over to check it out, and when one of the other lads reckoned he knew how to start it up we called his bluff; before we knew it the three of us were on the back of it and tearing through Cassiobury Park in total darkness. We obviously couldn't take it back so we hid it in some bushes before going home. The next evening we were kicking our heels and wondering what to do when we decided to see if the scooter was still there. As fate would have it, it was, and with Keith driving and me on the back we tore along the back lanes, whooping and laughing until I shouted for him to pull over and let me have a drive. He said to wait until the van behind had passed, and as I glanced round to check it out I was more than a little perturbed to see it was a police van, in all probability on its way to pick up the very scooter we were on. I shouted into Keith's ear to advise him it was the 'Old Bill', whereupon he promptly panicked and skidded into the side. We jumped off and ran but the two officers in pursuit must have been members of the Metropolitan Police track and field team because, despite our best efforts, they were onto us in no time at all. I was unceremoniously rugby tackled and thrown into the back of the van, followed closely by Keith. We were taken to the Police Station where I was duly charged with aiding and abetting taking without owner consent, driving without insurance and driving without a licence. My parents were summoned to come and collect me, and you can believe me when I tell you that the trip back home with my father was far from pleasant, in fact I can still remember him ranting at me, "Sign you up for nine years? I should have signed you up for bloody ninety! Have you got any idea of the shame you have brought on the family?" As it happens, this last remark was particularly ironic; what my father didn't know at the time, and I discovered only quite recently, was that when it came to bringing shame on the family my efforts didn't even come close. Apparently, his uncle, a certain Albert Bowes, applied for a driver's licence back in 1912 and in those days one had to produce evidence of good conduct and sobriety covering the previous three years. As he had recently been charged with drunkenness his application was refused. He felt aggrieved and decided to take the matter up with Sir Edward Henry the Chief Commissioner of Police for London and, with this in mind, on the evening of November 27th confronted him on the steps of his home. Sir Edward accorded him short shrift, so Albert calmly pulled out a revolver and fired two bullets into him at point blank range. On the 7th of January 1913 he appeared at the Old Bailey charged with attempting to murder the Chief Commissioner of Police. His sister, my grandmother Nellie Moxley, appeared as a witness for the defence where it emerged that the 25 year old barman had been invalided out of the army and then drifted from job to job. This failed to sway the jury who returned a guilty verdict and the court records show he was sentenced to fifteen years penal servitude. Albert was released from prison in 1922, and Sir Edward Henry, who had maintained an interest in his welfare, paid for Albert's passage to Canada to start afresh and live out the rest of his life in peace. Evidently he had some difficulty settling in as articles from The Florida Times-Union reported that, after terrorising a local family and following a gun battle, Albert George Bowes was shot dead by Sheriff Lyle near Live Oak, Florida on June 10, 1924. If my father thought I was bringing shame on the family with my little escapade I wonder what he would have made of his uncle's exploits.

The Florida Times-Union Jacksonville, Florida Wednesday, June 11, 1924:

"IN BATTLE OF BULLETS DESPERADO KILLED BY SUWANNEE'S SHERIFF"

WHITE MAN HAD SHOT DOWN H.C. MATTHEWS, MADE HIS WIFE AND DAUGHTER GET HIM FOOD, THEN WALKED AWAY.

FIRE ON NEIGHBORS; IS DROPPED BY SHERIFF

Total Stranger and Believed to Have Been an Escaped Convict - Was Evidently Demented - Had Money and Plenty Cartridges.

LIVE OAK June 10.--An unknown white man was shot and instantly killed this morning by Sheriff Lyle in attempting to effect his arrest. The man had shot and perhaps fatally wounded H.C. Matthews, a citizen of the Roseburg neighborhood, about ten miles south of Live Oak.

The man, a complete stranger, went to the home of Mr. Matthews last night at about 1 o'clock during a severe rainstorm and asked admittance. When Matthews opened the door, the stranger shot him down, using a .32 calibre automatic revolver. Following this, the man compelled Matthews' wife and daughter to build a fire and cook him a meal, threatening them with death if they did not obey him, and would not even allow them to give aid to the husband and father who was lying where he fell throughout the night. At about daybreak, the man ostensibly left the place, and Miss Matthews slipped away to the nearest neighbors, Lewis Lanier and Norman Brannan, for aid. When they arrived at the Matthews home the man was about the place and fired several shots at them but none took effect. Brannan came on to town for the sheriff.

Sheriff Shot First

Upon arriving at the scene, Sheriff Lyle organized the neighbors into a posse to run down the desperado. Soon he was discovered comming towards the group with his revolver in hand. He deliberately walked to within range of Sheriff Lyle, then dodged behind a big pine stump and took deliberate aim at the sheriff, but the officer was too quick on the trigger and fired, using a high powered rifle. The man was hit just above the eyes and death was instantaneous.

This occurred about 9 o'clock and soon Judge Dickert was on the ground and empannelled a jury, which, after viewing the body and hearing the evidence, brought in a verdict that the man came to his death from gunshot wounds at the hands of Sheriff Lyle, in the discharge of his duty.

Possibly a Convict

The man was aged about thirty years. He was a total stranger in this section. He was in his shirt sleeves and wore brown trousers and had on two shirts, the top one a blue striped madras and the under a blue denim. His shoes were heavy work shoes

14

Come the day of my appearance at Watford Juvenile Court, I had grown my hair out of the skinhead style and put on my Sunday best in an effort to look like a decent young man. I am not sure if it worked but the magistrate, in his wisdom, saw fit to let me off with a fine, a few endorsements and a six month driving ban. For someone who was not yet old enough to hold a licence, couldn't drive anyway, and had no intention of getting a car, this was not a major problem. The fine was more of an inconvenience; I spent all week delivering papers for W.H.Smiths and then had to take my wages down to the court, but at least I'd avoided reform school and that was a major plus.

It soon became obvious to all concerned that I needed to seek pastures new, and so it was that three months after my 16th birthday I found myself, in the early hours of a December morning in 1969, struggling up the gangway of an aging ship in Rotterdam. I'd joined the Merchant Navy. The vessel, the S.S. Hinnites, looked nothing like the one in the brochure. In fact, most of what happened over the next few years was nothing like

15

the brochure but, as I was to learn, nothing ever is. I'd like to say the crew and other officers were all friendly and made me feel at home, but they weren't and they didn't. Any camaraderie was solely down to the fact that we were all stuck on this rust bucket at the same time and it was easier to feign friendship than become a recluse. There was even an expression for it: 'Board of Trade Acquaintances', friendships for the duration of the trip.

It was a steep learning curve for a lad, a life changing experience where you were expected to learn fast and where there was little, if any, consideration shown. They had all gone through it and now it was your turn. You had to learn the vocabulary for a start, there was no left or right, it was port or starboard; no upstairs or downstairs, it was above and below; no walls, all bulkheads; no ceilings, only deckheads....and woe betide you if you got it wrong!

My first ship, S.S. Hinnites, 19,257t, Shell tanker (Kees Helder).

Great sport was also had at my expense and I fell for just about every trick played on first trippers. On the second day it was snowing on deck and I was wrapped up looking like someone off an Arctic convoy when one of the older apprentices sent me down to the engine room to get a 'long weight' off the Second Engineer. Of course, all the old hands have played these jolly japes since Noah went to sea so the Second took me to a little spot between the boilers and instructed me to wait there while he got the item in question. The heat was intense and within a short space of time I had taken off as many layers as I could while trying to retain some level of dignity. The sweat was pouring down my face when the Second emerged grinning like a Cheshire cat and said, "Well, you've had your 'long wait' you can go back up on deck now!" I hastened back up to the deck where I was met with an icy blast and half a dozen crewmates almost choking with laughter.

The following morning we were sailing across the Bay of Biscay on our way to Marseille and I was helping a couple of the crew clean up the deck when one of the AB's asked me to fill a bucket with water. I enquired where the deck taps were and was advised to just tie a rope around a bucket and throw it over the side. Ever keen to impress, I promptly tied several granny knots around the handle and threw the bucket over the side and into the North Atlantic which was speeding past at about ten knots. The bucket, the coil of rope, and very nearly my bloody hand, rapidly disappeared beneath the waves. I didn't need to turn round to know that I'd been stitched up, again. I finally wised up to these nautical jokes so when I was told to go and ask the storekeeper for some 'Jesus boots' so we could paint the side of the ship I felt confident enough to reply with a choice phrase of my own, "Only if they'll fit up your arse", and was subsequently left alone.

The ship docked in Marseille and as soon as I finished my watch I went ashore and headed for the nearest bar. Dock areas tend to have a life of their own, overzealous taxi drivers, seedy bars, loose women and an abundance of undesirable characters only too willing to separate you from your money. Look down the side streets and there is invariably a tattooist and a massage parlour within easy reach, Marseille was no different. I was to learn later that it was quite possible to escape the dock areas by grabbing a taxi into the heart of the cities themselves, which were usually vibrant and welcoming, but for the moment it was the red light districts that held a certain fascination for this sixteen year old. I had a couple of drinks and spent a lot of time just walking around the old town with no idea where I was going or what I was supposed to be doing. I was alone and, for all intents and purposes, lost. I was meant to be having a good time but didn't know where to start; I couldn't even chat to anyone in a bar because they were all speaking French! I wandered back to the ship for my watch and was almost relieved to be back aboard.

We left Marseille for Cyprus but within a couple of days I was bedridden with the shivers and sweats. There is no doctor on board ship so the Chief Officer usually fills the role; he examined me and came to the conclusion that he had no idea what it was and gave me a few pills on the off chance it might help. It didn't, and when we arrived in Cyprus a proper doctor was duly sent for who was none the wiser, gave me an injection and informed the Captain that I was not to be allowed ashore. Because I was having difficulty getting out of my bunk I was not banking on going ashore anyway but found the doctor's instruction a wee bit disconcerting. Whatever malady I had, Cyprus didn't want it, and a couple of days later we were bound for Tripoli; perhaps they might be more accommodating! We spent Christmas Day anchored off Tripoli and by this time I was back on my feet. Although I was now physically fit this was the first time I started to feel a bit homesick. Christmas tends to be a family occasion and I felt alone among strangers; doubts crept in as to whether I was cut out for a life at sea and I suppose I was just going through what most people do at that age but there was nobody to talk to about it. A good run ashore would sort me out, well, it would have if President Nasser hadn't been visiting Tripoli and all shore leave had been cancelled for political reasons. We were instructed to 'dress the ship' in flags in his honour and such was the contempt felt at having been denied a run ashore, the suggestion was put forward that we use them to spell out "Fuck off Nasser" right across the ship. For some, probably fortuitous, reason this was overruled! Tripoli was the first port where I felt aware of experiencing new cultures, just by watching the hustle and bustle on the dock, and the way the locals were dressed. An armed guard was standing at the bottom of the gangway and at certain times he would roll out a prayer mat on the floor and perform his ritual, usually accompanied by some choice phrases emanating from the crew on deck.

We discharged our cargo and sailed for Naples. As we approached the harbour a speedboat pulled alongside and a few swarthy looking fellows clambered aboard armed with empty sacks; in no time at all the sacks laden with duty free cigarettes and spirits were back in the speedboat, no doubt heading for some Mafioso's store. The local Customs officials were nowhere to be seen, and after watching 'The Godfather' some years later I can now more fully appreciate their reluctance to get involved; certainly our crew seemed well pleased with the result.

Naples lived up to all my expectations: the entrance into the bay was stunning, an array of buildings of all shapes and sizes ranging from modern to ancient seemed to start from the waterfront and work their way up the hill in no particular pattern, and all under the watchful eye of Mt Vesuvius. As soon as I finished my watch I was only too eager to get ashore and enjoy the delights on offer; another cadet and myself seemed to walk forever through all the narrow alleyways, up and down steps galore and passing so many old buildings I had the impression I was strolling through history. Add to this the natural characteristics of the Italians with their gesticulating arms and ultra smooth manner and the whole effect was quite intoxicating. However, there are only so many alleyways you can walk down before they all start to look alike; in fact we may well have been walking round in circles which would explain the similarities, and as the sun went down and darkness fell we felt a beer was in order. We found what appeared to be a welcoming hostelry and entered in anticipation. Although it was dark outside it was still relatively early in the evening and the only other customers were a couple of ladies, impeccably dressed in a sort of provocative manner, if you know what I mean. They were very friendly and came over to engage us in conversation. I was full of confidence as I was wearing the new double-breasted jacket that my father had purchased from an advert in the back of one of the Sunday papers; the ones that felt like a bit of sponge and didn't crease, I think it lasted about three weeks before all the stitching started falling to bits. Anyway, I was just about to suggest we ask the ladies if they wanted to find somewhere a bit livelier when they told us they charged a substantial number of lira for sex. At first I was not quite sure what they were getting at, their English was about as good as my Italian so it was all pretty hit and miss, but when they started acting it out, as if we were playing Charades, the penny dropped. As soon as they realised we couldn't afford what they were selling they left us, and I could see I was going to have to improve my technique considerably if I was to make any headway with the opposite sex.

In preparation for my continuing adventures afloat I flew home from Naples after just a month on the ship to start my course at Plymouth School of Maritime Studies: I was going to be a Navigating Officer.

I must go down to the seas again, for the call of the running tide, is a wild call and a clear call that may not be denied.

John Masefield

2
Plymouth

Most people who choose to go to sea do so with every intention of forging a career but once the reality of life aboard hits home, being away from loved ones, family and friends for months on end, many try to secure employment ashore. But the skills required to navigate a ship using only the sun and stars, face mountainous waves and hurricane force winds, load and discharge cargoes, splice ropes, read Morse code and pick out the constellation of the Seven Sisters on a cloudy night, are not usually in demand ashore. The options are strictly limited: either start a totally new career and suffer a substantial drop in income and status, or secure a teaching position at a Naval College. Those with an entrepreneurial spirit generally choose the former, those without often seek sanctuary in the prospect of an easier life in teaching. As a result, the majority of our lecturers possessed all the knowledge required on their particular subject but had minimal idea of how to impart it to others; this was a weakness which could be readily exploited by those of a certain disposition, such as enthusiastic young recruits.

Our class at college was called J23 and we rapidly established ourselves as a force to be reckoned with. There were about sixteen cadets from all over the UK and Ireland in J23, and a better bunch I could not have wished for. The majority of us had strong personalities and a shared sense of humour so a rapport swiftly developed that was to form the basis of lifetime friendships. There was Barry, slim and pale, he was as sharp as a tack and always looking to avoid any sort of work; his confidence inspired others but the reality was that his hormones were in overdrive and he would sell his soul for a girl, any girl. There was Patsy, a successful amateur boxer from Donegal who was carefree and far cleverer than he admitted; he had all the charm of the Irish and a smile that never left his face. Jimmy from Glasgow, short and swarthy with a slight stoop, was the old man of the class, eighteen years old and always acting the fool; we were half way through the course before we could understand what he was saying. I struck up a close relationship with Simon, we were the youngest in the group, and he always appeared to be intelligent and focused, although I was never entirely sure exactly what he was focused on. He recently told me that he enjoyed my company because he thought I could charm my way out of trouble and, on the odd occasion I couldn't, he felt confident I could punch my way out of it; I'm still not sure if that was meant as a compliment but either way it was certainly misguided. I have to mention Dick: he had the physique of a pipe cleaner, which only served to exaggerate his size eleven feet and make them look like flippers. This duly earned him the nickname Big Dick, a pseudonym that won him many admiring glances from the opposite sex and no doubt caused considerable disappointment in equal measure. Without listing them all, suffice to say there was no shortage of characters.

Every now and then, as you travel through life, you meet somebody special, a real 'diamond in the rough'. One such was Chief Tozer, a retired Chief Petty Officer from the Royal Navy who instructed us in the arts of drill and signals. He resembled a white Mike Tyson: his head was shaved apart from a perfectly formed Brylcreemed quiff at the front, stiff enough to withstand a gale force 10. His daily anecdotes made Bernard Manning look politically correct and nobody was ever called by their name, instead, he gave people nicknames and, as you would expect, none were even vaguely complementary. When he stated that you could not call yourself a sailor until you'd had V.D., got a tattoo and steered the ship, and I wittily responded that all I had left to do was steer the ship, it was the beginning of a long, and hopelessly one-sided, relationship. My accent led him to give me the imaginative nickname of 'London', and on one occasion he pronounced that the worst two sorts of people on God's earth were Londoners and Cornishmen, and asked me if I agreed with him. When I had the temerity to suggest that, as he had been born in Torpoint just across the River Tamar, he was effectively a Cornishman himself, he went into a defensive rant about how his poor mother had tried her damndest to get on the ferry to Plymouth and I shouldn't hold it against her! He gave us informal lectures about health: "They call them crabs 'cos they look like crabs under a microscope!"; women: "There are two types of women, women you fuck and women you marry!"; and the intelligentsia: "They can work out the specific gravity of a jar of pickles but haven't got enough common sense to figure out how to get the top off!". At the time we all laughed but maybe he wasn't too far out. He used to tell us how, when he first went to sea, he was seduced by a lady of the night and, as he was following her upstairs to her boudoir, he suddenly remembered what his mother had told him to do to fight temptation, and he said, "Devil, get thee behind me!"....which apparently the sod did and kicked him all the way to the top!

One morning at inspection Chiefy made some wisecrack about the length of my hair and ordered me to get it cut. It was no longer than anybody else's but he got a kick out of taking the Mick and I just happened to be the one in the firing line that day; it was nothing personal. Despite being naturally rebellious it was always difficult trying to get one over on Chief but this time he gave me an opening; if he wanted it cut, he would get it cut. That evening I shaved the whole lot off with a razor. The following morning as he was making inspection he stopped in front of me: he could plainly see, despite me having my cap on, that no hair at all was visible. As he placed a finger under the peak of my cap and pushed it up you could hear the sound of muffled laughter coming from the rest of the lads, he smiled broadly and in a heavy Cornish accent said, "Smart son, fuckin' smart".

The joke's on me, Simon (R), Plymouth, 1970.

Setting the fashion, Patsy (L) and me, Plymouth, 1970.

When I arrived in Plymouth my first impressions were not favourable; it was very much a military town and unfamiliar to me. Being the largest naval base in Western Europe inevitably meant the place was swamped with sailors, but when you throw three commando bases and an RAF camp into the mix, then add the Royal Navy training establishment, H.M.S. Raleigh, and about five hundred Merchant Navy cadets, you could see straight away that the competition for women was going to be extremely fierce. This was the first problem. The other was that Plymouth was culturally some years behind London, and the local dress reflected a style that had long since become part of history elsewhere. In addition, the natives regarded those from 'up the line' almost as hostiles from another planet who were solely intent on stealing their women, so they weren't entirely out of touch.

The city itself had been virtually flattened during the Second World War; its strategic importance during the Battle of the Atlantic had made it a prime target for the German military and they launched fifty nine bombing raids against it. After the war it was completely rebuilt with wide, modern boulevards stretching all the way from the railway station up to Plymouth Hoe. Luckily, the historic Barbican area, with its cobbled streets and narrow lanes leading down to the fishing boats, survived the worst of the bombings and was restored to some of its former glory. At the other end of town, another street also managed to escape the worst of the devastation and went on to become almost as famous as the Barbican, but for totally different reasons: the now infamous Union Street, known to sailors the world over and soon to become my second home.

Thanks to the Luftwaffe, there were now three distinct drinking areas within easy walking distance of each other and all offering their own unique style of entertainment. If you wanted a cosy drink in an old fashioned, waterside pub steeped in history, then it had to be the Barbican: it was the ideal place to sweet talk a member of the opposite sex. If a couple of pints in good company and a juke box playing the latest hits was what you wanted, the city centre was just the ticket. Should your desire be for ten pints of bitter, bad language, girls dressed in a manner which left nothing to the imagination, and a better than even chance of getting into a scrap, it had to be Union Street. Union Street was largely constructed during the Victorian era and was originally home to the wealthy, which explains the grand architecture and baroque styling of many of the buildings, such as the New Palace Theatre. It originally had trams connecting the city centre and the naval dockyard at Devonport, but since those heady days the street had evolved to become the hub of the city's nightlife and a flourishing red light district. There were so many pubs there that the 'street pub crawl' was attempted on a weekly basis but never actually completed. The names have long since passed into local history. The United Services, a scrumpy house of renown with barrels of the stuff on the back shelf, a haze of cigarette smoke which, over the years, had turned the plaster yellow, and which sold rough cider for one shilling and four pence a pint. Well and truly pissed for four bob, twenty pence in today's money: even Aldi can't match that! You'd struggle out of there and into Diamond Lil's where a fat drag artist would be gyrating on a stage the size of a table: in fact it probably was a table. The girls in there were so rough it wasn't always easy to pick out the drag acts from the customers, particularly after a couple of pints of scrumpy. There were too many pubs to name here, but without exception they all had something to commend them, whether it was dancing on the tables in the Beer Keller or listening to a gin-fuelled granny singing "White cliffs of Dover" in the Great Western Bar, there literally was never a dull moment.

This was the point in time when my lifelong relationship with beer began. In truth, I had dabbled a wee bit already, a few pints in backstreet pubs where the landlords were desperate for business, but nothing on the scale of which I was now embarking. I had learned that this amber nectar could take away all your insecurities, doubts and cares for a few hours. Now I had money and had left home there was nothing to stop me drinking my fill and more, and, as a seaman, it was expected of you. There was no shortage of other lads equally eager to take their fill at the numerous hostelries in a valiant effort to establish their credentials and, if at all possible, pull a girl at the same time. The drinking part was easy, although keeping it down sometimes proved tricky, but pulling a girl proved nigh on impossible.

The six months at college flew by; we got away with murder. We used to get a private, old fashioned double-decker bus from the college in town to the sports field a few miles away at Ernesettle and, as it slowly climbed the hill on the return journey, we'd jump off and run alongside then jump back on at the last moment as it picked up speed on the flat. I can still picture the face of one cadet, Tim, as he vainly attempted to regain his place and we all kicked out to stop him. We could hear him cussing from the top of the hill as the bus relentlessly drove on; it took him over an hour to get back. Tim had already decided against a career at sea and left shortly after that incident; I met him many years later working as a DJ in a Torquay nightclub. Sport training was always easy to kick into touch. The coach would check the register and a muffled, "Here!" would come from the dressing room as each name was read out. According to the register we'd have enough bodies to fill two teams but by the time those present actually reached the pitch there was barely enough for a game of five a side!

Our first signals lecturer had one foot in the grave. He would make his way to the front desk, take off his trilby and, without a word of acknowledgement, start tapping away at the Morse key in front of him, expecting us to write down the letter that was flashing on the wall behind his head. After a few of these solemnly silent rituals, we loosened the bulb so it wouldn't flash, and when his customary tapping left us unmoved, he was not quite sure what to say. The impasse continued for some minutes, as we sat motionless and secure in the knowledge that the old duffer would eventually have to react and feel rather foolish, as intended.

Seamanship was another breeze. The lecturer stood at the

edge of the water like Bligh barking instructions from the deck of the Bounty, "You will row out to the red buoy, round the green buoy, come back alongside, toss and boat your oars, then change coxswain and do it all again." Simple.....or so he thought. It was a freezing January morning, so we rowed straight across Sutton harbour to the Barbican, tied up to the Mayflower steps and, following the trail blazed by the Pilgrim Fathers, went straight into the Acropolis Cafe for a warming coffee. As we sipped our Nescafe we heard the faint tones of the lecturer's voice drifting across the oily water, "You'll swing for this, you bastards!" Despite our best efforts, he never developed a sense of humour; no wonder he left the sea.

Physics. Now that was a treat. We had our lectures in the main Polytechnic, given by a proper academic. Although he knew his subject well he had a lot to learn about us. The lesson was meant to start at one o' clock but we managed to convince him that we were allowed fifteen minutes banking time and did not need to start until one fifteen. He readily accepted this so when we pushed for one thirty, we got it. On one occasion in the lecture hall, as he stood with his back to us chalking equations on the blackboard, a large spitball of well chewed paper hit with a loud thwack and stuck about six inches from his hand. He launched a tirade against us for being so pathetic and we were to be punished with no coffee break! Nobody owned up to this childish prank but the trajectory meant that Big Dick was the prime suspect. When it got to break time we all started murmuring and coughing, "Coffee", louder and louder, until we could no longer be ignored and, finally, the lecturer relented saying that as long as we behaved ourselves we could go for our break! I have a lasting memory as he passed from workstation to workstation in the laboratory, diligently overseeing our experiments, when one joker attached a wire lead with a crocodile clip to the back of his jacket. As he moved slowly around, each of us took our turn to add another clip to his lengthening tail until about fifteen feet of wire trailed along behind before he realised, surreptitiously unclipped himself, and kept walking as if nothing had happened. But we all saw, and he knew we saw! Looking back, our treatment of him seems heartless, but we were only sixteen and he really should have established his authority over us. We would never have done anything like it to Chief Tozer!

It was the college's remit to make officers of us and to this end they had devised various testing expeditions which involved long distance rowing and arduous days hiking and camping on Dartmoor. My first task was with a classmate, Barry, and a senior cadet a couple of years ahead of us whose name escapes me. We were driven to the Dartmoor Inn at Lydford, then given directions and rendezvous points to follow on our return journey by foot. The senior cadet decided we should pitch the tent, cook the evening meal and plan the journey, but Barry and I decided we'd hatch a better plan from inside the pub. We sank a few ales and the landlord agreed to let us sleep in his barn; that was the first night sorted. Next day we had to hike across north Dartmoor to the Two Bridges, near Princetown, no problem for Barry and myself but the portly senior cadet made heavy weather of it. The conditions on Dartmoor can be demanding at the best of times, unforgiving tussocks of grass disguise the fact that there is often a foot or more of bog beneath, bogs that can stretch for hundreds of yards in any direction. Lumps of granite lay concealed waiting to twist an unsuspecting ankle while streams and rivers tempt you to use the granite rocks as stepping stones without any inkling of how slippery they are. There's the weather to consider: in no time at all clouds can roll in and you can be enveloped in thick fog concealing everything, and making it virtually impossible to navigate. On the plus side, there are some beautiful pubs on the moor and when the sun is shining you'd be hard pushed to find more scenic views anywhere.

We finally logged in that evening at the Two Bridges, another pub. Barry and I started sampling the goods while the senior cadet was bleating on about pitching the tent, again. I tried to point out that I had never pitched a tent before and could not be bothered to learn now, and it was dark to boot. He was

Grimspound & Warren House Inn distant, Dartmoor (James Penman).

adamant so we told him to go ahead; we had spotted a barn up
the road that would serve our purposes and we arranged to meet
up with him the next morning. That night Barry and I almost
froze in the barn: one of our sleeping bags had got soaking wet
so we had to throw the dry one over both of us. It was a
nightmare, and when we finally saw a light on in the farmhouse
we went and knocked on the door and asked if we could warm
up; I still can't believe we had the cheek so you can imagine how
cold we must have been. The farmer's wife was an absolute gem:
far from being shocked at a pair of shivering strangers at her
door in the early hours she invited us in, made us a steaming mug
of coffee and a huge bacon sandwich each. After another mug of
coffee we departed in high spirits, completely revived and with a
new found faith in human nature, to meet up with Grumpy. He
was looking decidedly pale around the gills and we faced a hike
right across south Dartmoor to Cornwood for our next
rendezvous. When we finally arrived, he was in a parlous state
and just wanted to pitch the tent and sleep, as usual. Cornwood
may be a quiet hamlet but thankfully it does have one redeeming

feature, the Cornwood Inn, and it was time to get acquainted. At closing time, Barry and I headed straight to the resting place for our last night on the moor which we had sounded out earlier in the evening, the public toilets! Not the most comfortable night I've had, but certainly unforgettable!

Our next task was to pick up a cutter from Plymouth's Sutton harbour and, along with a few others, row about 20 miles up the River Tamar to Morwellham Quay. At that point, three of the crew were to engage in an exercise up on the moor and the remaining three had to stay with the boat and monitor the tidal flows for a couple of days. Barry and I decided we had done our share on the moor so we insisted on staying with the boat, along with another of our classmates, Smoothy Jack. I never understood why he was called 'Smoothy' as his most noticeable trait was his speed, or to be more accurate, his distinct lack of it. Whatever it was, he took so long to make a decision, any decision, that the eventual conclusion was rendered worthless by the fact that the original options were no longer available. One example was at the evening meal at college; whoever was on serving duty at night would always try to ensure that his table was well provided for if there were any leftovers. I remember Simon coming over with a plate of leftover sausages, but by the time Jack had decided an extra sausage would be well received, we had already eaten them. While a sausage may seem of little importance, his reticence to jump in feet first had more serious drawbacks: by the time he had decided to give a girl he fancied the benefit of his company at a disco, she was already swapping tongues with the competition.

Once the boat was unloaded and the hiking trio had left, Barry, Jack and I decided that a little excursion to The Boot Inn at Calstock was in order. This entailed a quick crossing of the river and, as we had a boat and the river was narrow at this point, we did not anticipate any problems. If we had been a bit more observant with our tidal readings we might have noticed that the Tamar has an exceptionally strong flow and, at Morwellham at low tide, the banks are heavy with silt. We hatched a plan: Barry and I would row and, as soon as we hit the other side, Jack would jump ashore with a rope, which seemed pretty straightforward, if slightly naïve. As soon as we left the bank the tide quickly swept us downstream and Barry and I were struggling to make headway. Finally we got within spitting distance of the opposite bank and yelled frantically for Smoothy to jump. In fairness to Jack he did voice his concerns, but when eventually he realised that the alternative was to be swept miles downstream from our destination, he jumped into the gathering twilight and, fortunately, landed on the bank. Unfortunately, he sank instantly to his waist in the thick, soft mud. By the time he'd leant forward to drag himself and us off the water he looked and smelled like the monster from the deep. Of course, Barry and I were in stitches, and when I pointed out to Jack that he'd have to wait outside the pub because they'd never let him in dressed like that, he missed the joke entirely. As it was, we drank so much that I can't remember the return crossing, but the look on Jack's face when he sank into the mud will be with me to the end!

We had also developed a cunning plan to get back to base in record time: instead of waiting at Morwellham for the three cadets who were hiking on the moor, we had prearranged to start rowing on the ebb tide and meet them 5 or 6 miles further downstream. We arrived in plenty of time and carefully secured the boat at a beautiful riverside pub, the Spaniards Inn. It was our intention to have a couple of beers while waiting for slack water, the short period between tides when there is no tidal flow, before crossing the river to pick up the others. Time passed supping beer and gloating over our clever plan until we observed through a window that a crowd had gathered by the riverside, doubtless admiring the sleek lines and craftsmanship of our cutter. We finished our drinks and wandered nonchalantly over, eager to share our newly acquired nautical knowledge and understanding of tidal movements with our audience, and then stood quietly among the onlookers on the quay watching our boat as it dangled in mid-air, suspended by its mooring lines about four feet above the fast-flowing river and rapidly falling tide.

Our exploits had not gone unnoticed by the senior staff and after a riotous six month term our class tutor informed us that, as a direct result of our behaviour, we were to be split up and brought back separately for our next phase at college. We never stopped to consider the implications of this decision: we were young, exuberant and hungry for life's adventures. But the college staff were true to their word and some of the lads I never saw again, though I can still picture their faces even now, especially Patsy from Donegal: we had shaved our heads together and were particularly close. It would be forty years before he and I would meet again. We were all off to sea, and not just for a few weeks this time: this was the real thing.

I heard a voice within the tavern cry, "Awake, my little ones, and fill the cup, before life's liquor in its cup be dry."
Omar Khayyam

3
The S.S. Vexilla

Two weeks later and I was flying out to Singapore with Barry and Simon. We landed late in the evening and checked into Connell House, an old building that exuded character and invoked memories of colonial days long gone, and which now served as the Seamen's Mission. From the large rooms with their ceiling fans slowly rotating in a valiant struggle to assuage the heat, to the chit chats (lizards) running up the walls, it all seemed slightly surreal. After a quick wash and brush up we decided to venture out. The Mission bar was homely and inviting, the walls were adorned with ships crests and the handful of ancient mariners sipping Tiger beers and swapping yarns looked as much a part of the fixtures and fittings as the décor. All well and good for old salts but not for us: we headed for the bright lights. After a few cold beers in seedy bars we ended up in the early hours at the infamous Bugis Street. Barry and Simon had both lived in Singapore and knew what it was infamous for; I, on the other hand, did not. We had only just sat down and started drinking when I noticed a very attractive Chinese girl staring at me and licking her lips in such a suggestive manner that it could only mean one thing. This was an offer too good to refuse and I nearly tripped over Barry in my haste to introduce myself to the young lady before she got away; I didn't realise at the time that it wouldn't have mattered if she had got away because there were plenty more all bursting to make my acquaintance. I also didn't realise that they weren't actually girls, more girly boys, or to be completely accurate, boys. They were known as Kyties. With all these Kyties making designs on us, the numerous peddlers sticking everything from fake watches to toys in our faces, and the young children taking all our change by beating us at noughts and crosses, it was pretty chaotic. Bugis Street was on a cross roads; at night the roads were closed and tables and chairs were set up while street vendors managed to cook everything from lobster to stir-fried squid. The humidity and heat only added to the atmosphere, the vast majority of customers were either military or seamen of all nationalities; there were a few tourists but this was before tourism became the massive global industry it is today. I was to travel far and wide but never came across anywhere that came close to Bugis Street for sheer magnetism, an opinion I know to be shared by many. The sun was beginning to rise as we made our way back to the Mission.

Lobster supper, me (L), Simon and Barry (R), Bugis Street, 1970.

A couple of days later we flew on to Manila where we were booked into another hotel. It seemed only natural to get out and see what this wonderful city had to offer despite being warned that it was, at that time, known as the murder capital of the world. Sixteen murders a day apparently, although as we wandered around the seafront and shops we failed to see what all the fuss was about. However, as night fell the atmosphere changed: outside many of the shops men slept on camp beds with shotguns and there was even a sign on one bar instructing customers to leave their firearms at the door. Well, if there was going to be trouble we'd best be prepared, or so we thought, and to that end we each bought what were called butterfly knives. The blade is enclosed safely between two handles but when you hold one side of the handle and flick, the other handle comes round in a full circle, thus exposing the blade and joining up to make a fighting knife. We sat over our beers practicing the flick so we'd be ready when needed; we thought we looked like something out of a Clint Eastwood western but in reality we probably looked more like the Three Amigos! Thankfully, these new skills were never put to the test and the knives retired happily unused to a lifetime in the sock drawer.

The following morning we were driven across the island to the port of Tabangao and as we turned the bend in the road we looked down on a picture postcard scene: a beautiful, new ship anchored in a pristine, sun drenched bay with a backdrop of palm trees. "Lucky us" we thought, or not, as it turned out. Our ship was berthed just out of sight and in need of a decent coat of paint, which no doubt we would end up applying in due course. We signed on aboard the S.S. Vexilla and set sail the following day for Yokohama. Japan: the name alone suggested the essence of the Orient. The mood had been set as we sailed up the Japanese coast: Mount Fuji dominated the horizon and with its almost perfectly shaped cone topped with a covering of snow it was easy to see why this symbol of Japan held such spiritual significance. It became a constant companion over the following months and I never tired of its presence.

Simon and I were both on the four to eight watch; by ten past we had showered and changed and were ready to hit the town. We ran down the gangway straight into a waiting taxi where the driver asked if we were looking for a 'good time' and, like innocents abroad, we nodded eagerly. This was how, despite

Yokohama being a modern, thriving city, we ended up in another seedy bar in the backstreets. I could see a theme developing that was to continue throughout my life, but more of that later. We went in and were ushered to a table; there were plenty to choose from as we were the only customers. We ordered a couple of beers and before our eyes had become accustomed to the light, or lack of it, we had been joined by two lovely young Japanese girls. They motioned for us to buy them a drink each and it seemed perfectly reasonable; Simon thought Christmas had come early but after my Bugis Street experience I was a bit more suspicious. They spoke hardly any English but what few words they did speak left little to the imagination. "You want fuck fuck?" Simon was already half out of his seat at this offer but I managed to convince him that we had only been off the ship ten minutes and the least we should do was check out the town a bit, we could always come back. Simon took some convincing that we might find a better offer elsewhere but finally agreed to try. The girls persuaded us to buy them another drink before we went and, being sociable fellows we were happy to oblige. I walked up to the bar to settle the bill and when the barman told us the amount I thought he must have made a mistake. When I queried it he pointed to the bar tariff, specifically at the 'hostess drinks', and it was then that, being the smart lad that I am, I realised we were in deep trouble. Deciding to brazen it out, I puffed out my chest and tried, as best as the average sixteen year old is able, to look like a cockney hard man, laughed at the barman and refused to pay. He just tapped on the door at the back of the bar and out came the biggest Japanese man I had ever seen: he was built like Odd Job from the Bond films, wide as a barn door and with a look on his face that suggested he was hungry and we were on the menu. So, that is how Simon and I spent two week's wages in ten minutes and were back on board early for our watch. Of course, we had a lot to learn about life, but I can assure you I never fell for that scam again, although there were plenty more that I did fall for!

Our next port of call was Kobe, an altogether more

enjoyable experience. Japanese cities were years ahead of London, they were brighter and cleaner with a distinct lack of drunks or beggars. I'm not saying they didn't have any, but you seldom saw them; in the early 70's Japan was riding high and the wealth was readily visible. The restaurants had plastic models of their menu displayed in their windows, along with the prices, but these were not pathetic look-alikes, they were works of art that were striking in their brilliance. I think it would be fair to say that almost no-one I encountered ashore spoke more than one or two, if any, words of English, so these plastic replicas were ideal as all I had to do was point to what I wanted. In any restaurant, in fact state of the art coffee shop would probably be a better description as I never went in for anything more than a snack, it was common practice that as soon as you were seated you were served with a steaming hot, rolled flannel and a glass of iced water, even if you were only having an ice cream. The service could never be faulted and, compared to the way you were treated back home, it was a different world. Over the following months, we became regular visitors to Kobe, Nagoya, Yokohama and a host of other cities stretching as far south as Tokuyama and as far north as Muroran, and my respect for the people and culture of this great country continued to grow.

Up to now it had all been a bit of a holiday but things were about to change. We discharged our cargo in Kobe and during our passage to Singapore we had to prepare the ship for dry dock while at sea. Every tank had to be spotless to enable welding repairs to go ahead, and, as we had been carrying heavy, waxy oil, this was no easy task. I won't bore you with all the rudiments of tank cleaning but in those days it involved huge hosepipes, boiling water and a lot of hard graft, but for one reason or another some of the tanks were proving tricky. As a consequence the cadets and crew were split into two groups and worked four hour shifts non-stop, shovelling the dregs into rubber buckets, hoisting them up manually from the bottom of the tanks, and recycling the contents over the side. This went on for days until finally we reached Singapore and dry docked.

Singapore was an experience all of its own, you could smell the island from miles out at sea, and it always reminded me of a bowl of sweet, over ripe fruit. Jurong dry dock was something else altogether; the first thing you noticed was that the local labour force, referred to in those days as coolies, were all over the ship like locusts. The women had the worst of all jobs, cleaning out the insides of the boilers, but the whole place was a hive of industry. I wandered down to the shore canteen for a coke and at the table opposite me a worker was eating what I can only presume was a chicken with his fingers and just tossing the bones over his shoulder onto the floor where they were being gnawed by a rat the size of an average cat.

Anyway, the prospect of a few days loafing in Singapore bucked us up no end, until we met the new Chief Officer, usually just called the Mate. He had other ideas and it was his stated intention to knock us into shape, a shape of his choice, over the coming months. He had the air about him of somebody not easily impressed; he was slouched at the shoulders after years of staring out of bridge windows, with a stomach that betrayed his love of food. His receding blonde hair was styled in the mould of Bobby Charlton and the merest breath of wind would send a six inch lock heavenwards, but his tough demeanour ensured that nobody laughed. Of course, we didn't share his utopian views of work at sea and plotted to usurp his authority whenever an opportunity arose. Let me tell you from the outset, and without hesitation, that he won nearly every encounter by a country mile. It was an embarrassingly one-sided contest although we did offer as much resistance as we could muster. As with all natural leaders, he started as he meant to go on. First day aboard he took Simon, Barry and I down into the pump room, the very heart of a tanker and a snakes wedding of pipes and valves going in every direction. We had no idea what did what or where it went. He, on the other hand, climbed under the pipes, over the pipes, round the pipes and I swear, if he could, he would have gone through the damned things. Finally, he turned to us and asked us if we now knew what each pipe and valve did. Well, you can guess our answer, but there's only so much bullshit you can stack on one pile! His response was short and sweet, though nonetheless very effective: he informed us that after leaving Singapore we would not be allowed ashore again until we had produced a diagram of the pump room which included all the pipes and valves and what they did! I have always been challenged by anything that involved precision or dexterity so, while Simon and Barry produced excellent plans, my pathetic attempt was out of all proportion and earned nothing but derision from my so called friends. Nevertheless, it passed muster and that was all that mattered.

The Mate continued to stamp his authority on us at every opportunity. There are a series of rules which must be obeyed by all craft at sea. These rules are very precise and are, on average, about half a page or so long, they are called the 'Rules of the Road' and there are over 30 of them. They are fundamental to navigation at sea and must be known inside out. The Mate informed us that every Sunday morning he wanted us on the bridge to recite a new rule off by heart, word for word, and if we got it wrong there would be no shore leave for the culprit at the next port. Suffice to say we became fully conversant with these regulations by the end of the trip.

His next plan was another masterpiece. In order to have clean pipelines on a tanker they are flushed through with sea water, pumped up line A, down line B, back up line C and so on, like a map of the London underground, round and round and up and down, swinging valves right, left and centre as you go. Not an easy or pleasant task. At sea the cadets were meant to have Sundays as a study day to pursue their college correspondence courses; the Mate deemed that line washing was 'study' so most Sunday mornings were spent cleaning lines. By the time we paid off, we could have washed every line in our sleep, if required.

The cargo we were carrying was heavy and had to be heated to keep it fluid enough to enable it to be pumped ashore, so every morning the cadets' first job was to take the temperature of the oil in all thirty three tanks. This would appear on the surface to be a relatively simple task but the reality was somewhat different; firstly, the loaded ship had little freeboard and any wave of significance crashed across the deck necessitating a swift response to avoid disaster; secondly, the thermometers had to be lowered about twenty feet into the oil and left for a few minutes to get an accurate reading; last but not least, as you pulled the cord back up you had to squeeze the oil off it to prevent it dripping all over the deck and then wipe the gauge to actually read it through the muck, all the time keeping a sharp eye out for the next wave. Now, under such circumstances breakages are routine, but the Mate, and by now we were really beginning to warm to him, had come up with a way of addressing the problem. He advised us that the next cadet to break a thermometer would lose his shore leave at the next port! Well, there's only so much a cadet can take and we figured he was being unreasonable, but if he wanted no breakages, he would have none: unfortunately, he wouldn't get any accurate temperature readings either. As the thermometers carried on breaking we simply failed to report them to him and carried on going out every morning with broken ones and making the figures up. By the time we left ship only one thermometer remained intact; we'd finally got one over on him!

On our regular excursions ashore we had gained an insight into the romantic language of the local girls, "No money, no honey!", "Long time?", "Short time?", "Exhibition?", not the sort of stuff you find in the average phrase book but pretty self explanatory. Whenever we hit Singapore we invariably ended up on Bugis Street and as I had only just turned seventeen and was blessed with a baby face the gender bending Kyties showed more than a passing interest in me and on one occasion I was even ambushed in the toilet by one trying to convince me they loved me. It seemed to me that you could not go anywhere for a drink after midnight in Singapore without an attractive local woman displaying her charms in an effort to entice you to sample her wares; a weaker man would not have shown my restraint.

We once spent a few days in Pusan, now more commonly

known as Busan, the second largest city in South Korea after Seoul. The city now is a thriving hub of industry and commerce, an ultra-modern array of high rise towers that match any in the world, but it was vastly different back in 1971. Then, the sprawling layout seemed to lack any direction or planning but this in no way detracted from its appeal; the street markets, shops and bars lacked the neon signs so loved by the Japanese but what they lacked in glamour was more than made up for in authenticity and warmth. The Japanese treated foreigners with impeccable politeness, the Chinese were born to haggle and couldn't stop themselves trying to sell you something, but the Koreans gave me a welcome I would never forget; they were the Asian equivalent of the Irish. On my second night ashore I was in a traditional bar, heavy on the wood and light on fixtures and fittings, enjoying the local beer, OB 500, and wondering if my meagre resources would stretch to another, when a beautiful waitress arrived at my table with a fresh glass of beer. Before I could plead poverty she gestured that a gentleman at another table had paid for it, someone I recognised as the surveyor I had shown around the ship the previous day. He beckoned me over, treated me to a few more beers and offered to show me round Pusan the following day. Before I could make up my mind whether he was being extremely kind to a young apprentice or had designs on my nether regions, he explained that the waitress would also like to join us, which was as much a pleasant surprise as it was a welcome relief; it turned out to be one of the best runs ashore I ever had for a whole variety of reasons.

After another night sampling the delights of Pusan, I had about an hour to kill as I waited in the freezing cold near the ferry terminal for the liberty boat back to the ship, so I went into a local restaurant to get a coffee and defrost. It was distinctively oriental, with women in kimonos and very low stools around equally low tables. I stood out like a bare arse at Holy Communion: everyone stared at me. I had trouble making myself understood, even for a coffee, so when the waitress said, "Milk?" I just nodded politely and lowered myself uncomfortably onto a stool. She brought me a cup of hot milk accompanied by a small, egg cup sized bowl of sugar and, in my numbed state, I just emptied the lot into my cup, a gesture that was greeted with looks of dismay and a sharp intake of breath from the other customers. I was still thinking how odd this seemed as I lifted the cup to my lips and took a large gulp; whether or not they saw me wince I cannot be certain: it was patently not sugar in the bowl, but salt. I was now faced with a dilemma: do I screw up my face and leave with my tail between my legs or brazen it out? I decided on the latter course of action and drank just enough to look as though I had finished, paid the bill and left with my head held high, although as I walked out I heard the faint but distinct notes of muffled laughter.

On one occasion, an unexpected diversion took us to Durban, and I was ashore with Simon partaking of the local cane brandy, in quantities well in excess of government guidelines, when one of those ideas came to mind that often make an appearance as the end of one bottle approaches and the opening of another beckons. We decided it would be a good idea to jump ship and get a job on a safari park, and with the prospect of returning to ship for our cargo watch no longer a consideration, we started to imbibe with even more gusto and teamed up with a local drunk who announced that in return for us buying the drinks, he was happy to drive us round all the pubs in town. Although Durban is a large rambling city that stretches away from the coast like a wrinkled carpet through the hills and ravines of the hinterland, in the euphoria induced by cane brandy, such an optimistic venture sounded like a perfectly reasonable arrangement until we reached the seemingly inevitable outcome: a head on crash with a tree in the middle of a roundabout. We bade farewell to the driver and, following a minor altercation, found ourselves in a police van and on our way back to the ship which was now nearly empty and riding so high in the water that the gangway was an almost vertical plank lacking any rungs to support your feet. Somehow we managed to negotiate our way on board only to come face to face with the

Mate, who was surprisingly lenient toward our mumbled apology and informed us that we had orders to clean one of the main tanks in preparation for back loading some highly toxic substance. A couple of the cadets would do the tank cleaning and then the others would take care of the loading. This seemed a perfectly acceptable proposition until Barry, living up to his reputation as 'the mouse that roared', piped up and said that it was stupid and we should stick to our normal watches whereupon the Mate, not known for his easy going attitude towards cadets, decided that we would all do the cleaning and all do the loading. Hence my memories of South Africa were forever tainted by bottles of cheap brandy and three days without sleep. Once we were back at sea, we pumped all the toxic waste over the side and sailed on our way.

One of our tasks as we steamed up the African coast was to strip down the fairleads, the heavy rollers located along the side of the ship from bow to stern through which the mooring ropes are fed, clean and scrape them, then grease and refit them. Simon and I were working down the port side and a couple of new cadets who had recently joined were to starboard. The actual roller is very heavy and awkward to grip and negotiate back into position, which was proving tricky for us but not the other two who seemed to be skating along. Being made to look like a pair of bumbling fools by these newcomers was unacceptable. We established that the large, machined washer on which the roller had to sit was, now that it had been greased, sitting slightly proud and thus preventing us slipping the roller over it. It seemed to me that if the washer wasn't there then there would be no problem; the answer was staring us in the face: a quick flip, a distant splash and we were on our way. In no time at all we had overtaken the others, finished the job and re-established our superiority. We understood that with the passage of time the absence of the washer would eventually cause the fairlead to seize up, but by that time we'd be happily ensconced on a different ship and it would all be someone else's problem.

Our new orders were to proceed to Kharg Island in the

Persian Gulf and load a full cargo for Ceylon, now known as Sri Lanka. In the early 70's the cities of the Persian Gulf bore no resemblance to the metropolises of today; even Dubai was such a dismal sight that hardly anybody bothered to go ashore. There were no buildings of any grandeur, in fact I can't recall any that were more than one storey high, no chance of a cold beer either, and as for women, well, you'd be lucky if you so much as saw one. First timers to the Gulf were always told that there was a woman behind every tree, the joke being that there weren't any trees; they were so few and far between they were even marked on the charts as navigational aids. Kharg Island belonged to Iran and was a state of the art offshore oil terminal that could pump oil faster than just about any other port but, unfortunately for us, they were on strike when we arrived so we had to anchor up for a few days with forty or more other tankers, all waiting to feed the insatiable demands of the world's refineries.

When we finally got alongside the Iranians did their level best to make up for lost time and pumped so fast that the ship looked like she was sinking. We had two men going non-stop from bow to stern and back again tightening up the mooring ropes; within twelve hours we had loaded thirty thousand tons and were on our way. In those days there was little love lost between the locals and the sailors so there was a welcome sense of relief when we passed the Quoins, a small group of islands generally regarded by seamen as the entrance to the gulf, bound for a port that offered the prospect of some fun and laughter. Just over ten years later the Iraqi Air Force intensively bombed the Kharg facilities and by 1986 the pumping had stopped.

It is a common occurrence when a ship is steaming at night to produce bioluminescence, the action of the ship and propeller churning up the water exaggerates the natural light that radiates from certain species of plankton to such an extent that it looks as though somebody is shining a massive spotlight underneath the ship, and the ship's wake is like a ribbon of neon as it fades gradually into the distance. As we steamed slowly down to Ceylon we were treated one night to a particularly spectacular light show, the bioluminescence was unbelievably bright, almost milky white; it shames me now to think how I so readily took these wonders for granted at the time and didn't appreciate how lucky I was to witness them.

Our destination was Colombo, the old capital of Ceylon, a thriving city which carried the legacy of British colonialism in its many grand buildings, still standing proud among the sprawling local offerings despite the toll exacted by the ravages of time. Every other shop there seemed to sell gemstones and the natural sales ability of the Sinhalese resulted in me buying a pair of water sapphires at what I had been assured was a bargain price, but for which I had absolutely no use. They are probably still collecting dust in my sister's bottom drawer. We had a few days there and for once I actually did some sightseeing, wandering along the local beaches and among the Buddhist temples, restaurants and bars, which were all very beautiful but somehow lacked the excitement and glamour of Singapore that was so enticing to a seventeen year old sailor.

Once back in Southeast Asian waters we had another memorable run ashore, this time in Pulau Sambu, a small Indonesian island close to Singapore. We lay at anchor waiting for the pilot to take us alongside. I was on the bridge and once the pilot was aboard the Captain ordered the anchor to be raised. Unfortunately, he had not appreciated the speed of the rapidly ebbing tide and by the time the pilot reached the bridge we were fast aground and there was nothing we could do. As the tide continued to fall we were soon, literally, high and dry and could only sit and await the return of high water and the arrival of a pair of tugs from Singapore to get us off safely. That evening I went ashore with one of the new cadets, Andy, for a drink in the Seamen's Mission. The place was quieter than a vicar's fart at a funeral until a local came in and offered to take us to a nearby island that was full of women. Such a proposal obviously merited serious consideration so we enquired as to the price. I can't recall the precise figure that he quoted other than we felt it was exorbitant. Usually in such circumstances there is some competitive haggling and it is possible to play one offer against another, but not this time. We quickly devised a scheme, jumped into his dugout and set off into the darkness. It was an eerie feeling watching the shore lights fading behind us as the sea ahead grew choppy, but the promise of an island full of women gave us courage. Eventually we beached on a beautiful stretch of sand bordered by a few grass huts as music drifted across on the warm night air and reminiscent of a south sea fable, girls rushed out of the huts to greet us like long lost brothers, proffering beers and smiling sweetly. The Missions to Seaman could learn a lot from these people! Suffice to say that we enjoyed the hospitality of the locals before we bid farewell for the return trip. Back in our trusty dugout we set off in high spirits, waiting until we were sufficiently close to Pulau Sambu to swim if required should events take a turn for the worse. We put our plan into action, disputed the original amount we had agreed on for his services and suggested a more reasonable sum; well, more reasonable for us. He took umbrage at this and became increasingly agitated and threatening. We tweaked our plan: as soon as the canoe beached we ran hell for leather back to the ship. The boatman couldn't get into the dock area so we felt safe. The next morning he appeared on the jetty with a policeman, but as luck would have it, the policeman appeared to send him off with a flea in his ear, though I didn't bother going ashore again that evening! I felt guilty not giving him any payment but it had seemed to us he was trying to fleece us. This is one of life's amusing contradictions: when you feel you've been ripped off a few times you can easily begin to lose your faith and trust and start thinking everyone is a robbing bastard, but then end up doing the same to others! I heard recently that the other cadet is now a high level bank executive. Yes, life's full of irony too.

After nearly nine months, Simon, Barry and I paid off in Singapore and flew home for a well earned break. Much as I have castigated the Mate on this voyage, the truth is I owe him a debt of gratitude as he ensured that I knew all the basics necessary to do the job which made my future trips considerably easier.

And that inverted bowl we call the sky, where under, crawling, cooped, we live and die, lift not thy hands to it for help, for it rolls impotently on as you and I.

Omar Khayyam

4
Growing pains

After the initial euphoria of returning home had faded, which took about a day, I was keen to get out and about to see what, if anything, had changed while I'd been away. It didn't take long to realise that nothing had, other than me, and that my absence had gone largely unnoticed. I can't say I was surprised but there was an air of acceptance that things would never be the same again. Whenever I did bump into someone I knew there was usually a brief conversation about where I had been, followed by the inevitable, "When are you going back?" which, although not meant as such, only reinforced the impression that I was a stranger in my own town. I no longer felt I belonged there but, unfortunately, I was none the wiser as to where I did belong and, being unable to figure it out for myself, decided to concentrate on more serious pursuits, such as drinking and chasing women.

Although highly enjoyable, these two activities were time consuming and expensive, and the gap between my income and expenditure grew steadily wider. I was out every night: in Watford on the weekend there was plenty happening and, during the early part of the week when it was quiet, I'd get the train into London and go clubbing until the small hours. Wearing my quality, made to measure suit I'd purchased in Singapore, and drinking brandy American, I felt I cut quite a dash in the clubs of Soho, though no doubt others held varying opinions of this seventeen year old upstart. When the clubs had closed, I'd catch the paper train back to Watford and stroll up a deserted High

Street just as the town was beginning to wake. You get a completely different perspective on a place at the crack of dawn, like a blank canvas silently and patiently awaiting the grubby paws of an awakening world, before the peace and serenity rapidly evaporates as the traffic begins to flow.

I had grown out of my Skinhead apparel and matured, like all the others, into a Suedehead: my hair was that little bit longer and out went the boots and Levis to be replaced by two tone Tonic suits, tasselled loafers and Crombie coats. This new look was a definite improvement and my efforts on the social scene were beginning to pay dividends. I was living at a hectic pace, the time seemed to fly by and I was all too aware that my return to sea was imminent: not a prospect I viewed with any relish. Had I paused for a moment I may have noticed the correlation between having a good time and drinking; I may have stopped to consider why I spent every day and every night in some degree of inebriation, but I didn't: I was seventeen and had every intention of enjoying life to the full which, in retrospect, was an unachievable ambition.

On my last day at home my father expressed the feeling that he and mum were disappointed that I had chosen to go gallivanting every night rather than spend some time with them, and although I could see their point, I felt that whatever I did would ultimately be a disappointment to them. I was never going to live up to my father's expectations because we had such disparate views: he held a high regard for the law and the establishment while, even in those days, I saw the whole shebang as corrupt and greedy and wanted no part of it.

I seemed to have a natural talent for a dissolute lifestyle and would happily have carried on with my debauchery if the bank manager had been more accommodating, but time and tide wait for no man and after just five short weeks the shipping company sent me a telegram requesting that I report immediately to join the S.S. Hyala in Swansea. I have no personal grievance against Swansea but if it had been Honolulu at least it would have sweetened the pill a bit: I found it hard to get excited about

South Wales, and still do.

It was a miserable evening as I trudged up the gangway onto a manky old tub carrying black oil. I was shown to my cabin and advised that I would be on watch later that evening; I could hardly wait! We left Swansea and sailed for Greenock in Scotland: not much improvement, if any! The ship was then sent to Belfast for a major refit, also not at the top of my wish list at that particular time with 'the Troubles' just kicking off, but I thought there was a distant chance that it might prove interesting.

Leaving Watford had been made even harder as I had met a sweet young lady who was heartbroken at the thought of my sailing away for months on end. I suppose it was the first time I'd had a proper girlfriend and I viewed the prospect of being separated for eight months as deeply depressing. I imagined her out with other fellows and there was absolutely nothing I could do about it. These thoughts were eating me away and something had to be done: either jump ship, which I confess was very tempting, or finish with her altogether. It was while my mind was in this state of flux that I and another couple of lads went out for a few drinks. The Guinness was having the desired effect and we ended up in a sort of pub and folk club, the name 'White Heather Club' springs to mind but it's been too many years to be sure. Anyway, there was a great crowd in there and as the songs were very catchy, we joined in some of the choruses. One I remember well was 'The Black and Tans'. With the intoxicating combination of the Guinness, the Irish brogue, the roisterous crowd and lively atmosphere, I didn't have a clue what we were singing: in London a Black and Tan was a Guinness and Bitter and I knew nothing of the notorious Tans and their violent campaign to suppress the Irish! Later in the evening someone was singing a ballad but, as is often the case, it was difficult to make the words out and in my inebriated state I blurted out a comment to one of my mates which was overheard by a feisty young colleen who was sitting just in front of me. She turned in a flash and wanted to know if I was joking about their music, apparently the song was a tribute to an IRA martyr and she felt I was insulting him! Tricky, we'd obviously stumbled into the wrong bar and our accents were a bit of a giveaway! I mumbled a genuinely sincere apology, so she introduced me to her friends and we all got on well. When the pub closed the girls invited us to a nightclub and it would have been churlish to refuse. When the nightclub closed I offered to take her home; I didn't know at the time that she lived just off the notorious Falls Road and we had to go through an army checkpoint to get there. As we walked along she suggested I keep my mouth shut as we approached a few fellows on the corner but I'd already figured that out for myself. By the time we got to her house it must have been well after 2am, but all her family were still up. The house was terraced in the typical style with a small lounge in the front and living room at the back, so she asked me to wait in the front room while she explained to her family that I was a Brit. They obviously deemed it OK and I was led into the back room where a whiskey was thrust into one hand and a bacon sandwich into the other, and the party resumed. I slept what remained of the night on the sofa after Jeanette's father strongly advised against trying to get back to the ship before daybreak. So began my love affair with Ireland and its people. We were in Belfast for three weeks and the people were so friendly that I didn't want to leave. Jumping ship was also postponed indefinitely as I'd already dispatched my letter to the lass in Watford bidding her farewell and was ready for the open sea again.

The first few ports weren't particularly exciting: Ellesmere Port, Tranmere, Stanlow, and Southampton. I still felt there was something missing in my life, but rather than spend time analysing exactly what it was I decided to become a proper sailor and get a tattoo. Everybody had assured me that it wouldn't hurt so when we got to Southampton I just went to the nearest studio, tossed a coin over a smiling shark and 'Death before Dishonour' and, thankfully, the shark won. When the tattooist started pressing the electric needles into the top of my arm the pain kicked in and the blood started to ooze out; I almost quizzed him as to whether he knew what he was doing but didn't want to inflame the situation. I even considered stopping him there and then but if there's one thing that looks more ludicrous than a shark on your arm, it's half a shark.

The company I worked for had only two ships that were able to carry 'white wax', our next cargo, which had to be kept hot to maintain any sort of fluidity, and the main two ports for delivery were Swansea and New Orleans. The ship I was signed on had previously loaded the cargo in Curaçao and sailed for Swansea, but as luck would have it we arrived in Curaçao just as New Orleans needed a delivery: most fortuitous.

For cadets, the most important character on the ship is the Mate and we had a new one join in Belfast. His wife was around while we were in dry dock and it became immediately apparent that he was a thoroughly hen-pecked little Scotsman who thought very highly of himself. He came into our cabin one day and picked up a porno magazine that had been left by one of us on the table, smiling as he flicked through its glossy compendium of tits, bums, and exposed flesh. We smiled too because his wife had quietly entered through the open door behind him and looked over his shoulder. She heaped scorn and abuse on him and he turned bright red and slunk away. We all laughed, but he must have felt humiliated and in order to repair his damaged pride and attempt to erase the incident he set about reasserting his authority over us. It transpired that, as usual, I would be the one in the firing line. I'd come off the deck one afternoon and looked to see if there was anything to eat in the pantry, and there, between the cheese and jar of sandwich spread, was a tempting bowl of custard. I asked the second steward if it belonged to anyone and he advised me that it had been the Mate's supper a couple of days previously but he had obviously not wanted it, so if I didn't eat it, he would throw it out. Waste not want not is my motto so down it went: most enjoyable. A few hours later I was ordered to go and see the Mate on the bridge where I was promptly grilled over the whereabouts of his custard; I explained the situation honestly and apologised saying that if I had done anything untoward it was certainly not intentional. Not good enough, apparently! He felt it time to impose his authority over this cocky cadet and advised me that I would not be allowed ashore in the States. I meekly pointed out that I had asked the second steward and felt he was being a bit harsh in his punishment; I seem to recall him saying something about me having a lot to learn just before the red mist descended! I turned and stormed off the bridge and down to my cabin where the other cadets wanted to know what was going on. I was fuming and ranting about this 'pathetic little pip-squeak of a Mate' and how I'd love to give him a good hiding, when a quiet voice in a thin Scottish accent came from behind me saying, "You've got a very loud voice Mr. Moxley, I'll be reporting you to the company!" I just couldn't help myself and told him in no uncertain terms that he should "Fuck off out of my sight!" and advised him that I would also report him to the company over his inept handling of the "bowl of custard" saga to see what they made of his management style! Another fine mess I'd gotten myself into. However, my little rant had the desired effect: no more was said about it and he left me pretty much alone for the rest of the trip, although he did have a last attempt to slip the knife in but, unfortunately for him, it came to nought.

The next few months were spent running between Venezuela, Curaçao and the States. Curaçao is a most beautiful port to visit, it is one of three islands, along with Aruba and Bonaire, which used to be known as the Netherland Antilles and which were colonised by the Dutch in the 17th century. Willemstad, the main port and capital, has a natural, deep water harbour and although the buildings are magnificent examples of Dutch architecture they are painted in the bright colours usually associated with the West Indies. What makes this port so different from others is that, to enter the harbour, a ship must steam through a narrow canal that runs alongside the town centre and, as all the properties are facing the water, it gives the distinct impression that you are actually sailing through the middle of town. At the time, the population of the whole island was about

140,000 and this seemed to create an easy going atmosphere where everyone knew everyone else. It was the prettiest and friendliest Caribbean island I ever visited and I never tired of it.

Sailing into Willemstad, Curaçao (Julian@Soul Aperture).

Curaçao had many attractions apart from the climate and the laid back ambience. One particular favourite among visiting sailors was Happy Valley, a huge camp surrounded by wire, not unlike a prison camp, but with a couple of bars in the middle and more women than you could shake a stick at! Most sailors seemed to end up there for a few late drinks and to enjoy the banter with the girls. There is a long held myth at sea that if you are a 'Cherry Boy', a virgin, you should get the services of one of the women for nothing, but despite all my pleading and protestations, I couldn't negotiate even a small discount, never mind a freebie.

One run ashore in America was in a small port called Fall River, Massachusetts, and I have good reason to remember it well. The town itself was not exceptional and after a few beers I ended up in a backstreet bar, again, along with a few of the others off the ship. Beer had taken its toll on all of us which would not normally have been too much of a problem, but the rest of the bar was full of bikers. These were no ordinary bikers, these were real mean, tattoos on their faces mean, bikers. I distinctly remember one had a swastika in the middle of his forehead and the words 'Chosen Few' on either side. I made a mental note that if it kicked off it might be best to try to avoid him. The atmosphere deteriorated until it became noticeably dodgy and my bowels were telling me this was not a healthy place to be, but none of us wanted to show cowardice in front of the others, pathetic really. Anyway, I decided that if there was going to be trouble I would be better able to handle it with a few beers in me: about twenty seemed appropriate for the circumstances. As I waited for service at the bar a lady came and stood next to me, as if I didn't have enough problems, and she said that the gang had knives; they knew how to use them and planned to roll us for our money. This concentrated my mind marvellously, and then she said she had rung a taxi for us and it was going to hoot as soon as it got outside. I did my best to nonchalantly pass this information to the others and for the next few minutes, time passed in surreal slow motion. As soon as the horn sounded, we bolted out of there in one second flat and told the driver to get moving while he still had a car! It is only now, as I write this forty years later, that I realise what a debt of gratitude I owe that woman.

The rest of the trip was relatively uneventful; we called into numerous ports, from Houston, Texas to Norfolk, Virginia and Albany, New York, but in truth most of them were uninspiring places which, once seen, would be quickly forgotten. The one outstanding exception to this was New Orleans. It was always lively and I could be found drinking 'Hurricane' cocktails in the jazz clubs down Bourbon Street at every opportunity; you could see why it was known as the Big Easy. New Orleans lies about 100 miles up the Mississippi River from the Gulf of Mexico and the long river passage gives you ample time to absorb the atmosphere. There is nowhere else that compares; I remember one river pilot coming aboard wearing cowboy boots and hat, he calmly pulled down the bridge window, dragged the tall pilot chair over to it, pulled himself up onto it and rested his feet on the window sill before turning to the Captain and saying in a deep southern drawl, "OK Cap'n, give her the gun!". By the time we finally arrived at New Orleans to be greeted by a town whose architecture was a mind-blowing mixture of styles, from French Creole to Italianate, from Greek revival to Victorian and American colonial, and berthed alongside a paddle steamer that looked like something out of a film set, you knew you were somewhere special and bound for a good run ashore. It never disappointed.

I generally managed to keep myself out of trouble, which was more than could be said of the ship itself. It was old, rusty and riveted, and the rivets were leaking which, when you are carrying black oil and visiting ports way up river, is a problem; a big problem. We used to try fixing the leaking rivets on every ballast trip but it was a hopeless task. The worst episode that I can recall occurred during a visit to Martinique. We arrived at the port of Fort-de-France in the dead of night and dropped anchor. The rising sun revealed a bay of pristine beauty with the deep green foliage of the volcanic mountains rolling down and melting into the gently lapping turquoise water, where our ship lay serenely at anchor, surrounded by a slowly spreading ring of thick oil. Fearing yet another fine for pollution, the Mate had all of the cadets walking around the deck emptying watering cans full of detergent into the sea in an effort to disperse the slick and sink the oil; the moral of the story seemed to be that it was OK to pollute as long as it couldn't be seen.

So, disaster averted, or at least temporarily concealed, I ventured ashore to see what this small French colony had to offer its visitors. My first impressions were not favourable, and the beautiful setting could not change the bland nature of the town. The locals had inherited the language and arrogance of their colonial rulers but not their architectural style or culinary skills, or so it seemed to me. I wandered around town and took refreshment in a few bars in my desperate search for something to attract my interest, but to no avail. My pulse slowed. My eyesight dimmed. It was a wholly underwhelming experience.

By now, the Mate had been with us for about six months and was due to be paid off. On the appointed day for hand over, his relief arrived and I was in the office as the little bag of neuroses explained to his replacement the problems of leaking rivets and how we had tried to keep on top of the issue. As you can imagine an empty oil tank is very slippery, full of volatile fumes and very dangerous, and every ballast trip, when we were empty, the cadets had to climb down oil covered rungs and step across onto oil covered ledges to try and locate the leaking rivets which we had identified from ashore, and fix them with a kind of instant cement. All this time the ship would be rolling and none of us had safety harnesses. Once, and it was just the once, the Mate descended into one of the tanks, but he didn't have the courage to take the large step over from the ladder to the ledge, and he never came down again. You can imagine my contempt as the wee Scot calmly explained to the new Mate how he would stand on the ledge and, as the ship rolled, slide along to the bulkhead with his arms out as though he were on a tight rope! The saddest part is that I think he had convinced himself that he had actually done it.

Anyway, the new Mate was a diamond and we got on brilliantly: he was impressed with my ability and trusted me to do a good job. After a few weeks had passed, he asked me what I had done to upset the previous Mate as the report he had written on me was so damning. He told me not to worry unduly as the only report that went to the company was his, as the Mate when I paid off, and his would be rosy, which was a stroke of good fortune.

Another incident that I recall with affection was a visit to a small port in Venezuela called Caripito, about 70 miles up the Rio Grande. Dense jungle stretched all the way up river, and at the village the river was so narrow that it required the ship to execute a three point turn in order to turn around, in the process covering the fo'c'sle head with overhanging branches. The locals were selling parrots, monkeys, and even little crocodiles from their dug outs. I went ashore that night with an engineer cadet for a few beers and a couple of local lads asked us if we were looking for something a little livelier. As there was absolutely nothing of note in the village we said "Yes, please" and they led us through the jungle for some way, far enough for me to wonder whether we'd made a serious mistake. Suddenly, we emerged from the jungle into a spacious clearing with a huge mud hut in the middle. Our guides beckoned us to enter the dim interior, lit only by a few hurricane lamps dotted about, and, as my eyes slowly adjusted to the darkness, a voice came from one corner, "Bloody hell, Moxley, we wondered how long it would take you to get here!" It turned out half the ship's crew had beaten us there!

I and another cadet paid off in Curaçao after about eight months and were booked into the Avila Beach hotel. This was a beautiful hotel with a palm fronded bar on its own private beach, and about sixty yards offshore was a floating sun deck. The first night we got plastered and decided to swim out to the raft, we stripped off on the beach and dived in but after only about fifty yards I distinctly felt something bump against my leg. Something did not feel right and when I called out to Alistair he said he had also felt something in the water. We left the water sharpish, finished our drinks and went to bed. The next morning I went down for breakfast and a pretty waitress, who I recognised as the barmaid from the previous night, came up to me and said I must be very brave. I saw no reason to dispute her assessment but enquired how she arrived at that conclusion. She explained that during the day, with all the noise and splashing, the big barracuda stayed out at sea, but at night, when it is quiet, they come in to forage, along with a variety of other hungry marine life. I almost choked on my papaya, but managed a knowing smile to suggest I was not a man to be troubled by such minor inconveniences as feeding barracuda and their associates, although I never repeated that particular night time foray. She was obviously impressed because she insisted on taking me snorkelling to a local bay the next day to see an old wreck covered with coral. I'd never been snorkelling before and was mesmerised by the array of colours on display; I believe Curaçao is now one of the most popular diving destinations for precisely that reason.

The flight home was a nightmare. Alistair, a good friend, had received a Dear John letter from his fiancée while aboard and had waited until he paid off to drown his sorrows. He was an outstanding character for whom I held great admiration and I could not allow a man like that to drink alone. However, I could only manage a full bottle of brandy before passing out, so he had to struggle on alone with his second bottle of scotch. When we arrived in Amsterdam we were both at death's door, I only had to survive a short hop to Heathrow but poor Alistair had to get back to the north of Scotland. I had less than two weeks to recover before heading back to Plymouth for my next phase at college.

The worldly hopes men set their hearts upon, turns ashes –
or it prospers; and anon, like snow upon the desert's dusty
face, lighting a little hour– is gone.
Omar Khayyam

5
At sea

I had a couple of weeks at home before I was due back in
Plymouth for my next period at college, so I made the best of it
in customary style. It was fast approaching Christmas and
everywhere seemed to be festooned with lights, the sounds of
celebration, and pubs packed with revellers. I busied myself
making a handsome contribution to their coffers. The highlight
of the holiday was New Year's Eve, dancing on top of the
fountain in Trafalgar Square and singing Auld Lang Syne before
almost freezing to death as I sat shivering on the train back to
Watford in my soaking wet clothes. I was still recovering a
couple of days later at Paddington station, and as I searched the
departure boards for the next service, having just missed my
intended train, I heard a familiar voice in my ear, "Alright, John?"
It was Simon; this would be a long journey and we had a lot of
catching up to do; it was a good job the bar was well stocked.

The next six months were a breeze compared to life aboard
ship and, although the original class had been split up, there were
still enough of us ready and willing to put on a decent
performance as circumstances permitted. However, there was no
denying that we had matured after eighteen months at sea and, as
a consequence, the lecturers escaped the worst of our pranks and
excesses.

I was now eighteen and had every intention of making the
most of what I considered to be an additional six months paid
leave. After spending so long in the company of women who
were often only interested in the contents of our wallets, now

women were in abundance and freely available. Never wishing to miss any opportunity, we were out every night. Officially, we were meant to be in by eleven and the door would be locked by half past, but this was a minor inconvenience and just meant that we had to climb through one of the downstairs windows. At the weekends, I think it would be fair to say that as many came in via the window as the door, but nothing was ever said. The downside to this nocturnal frenzy was that some of us were permanently knackered and it was not unusual to find a swathe of the class asleep during a lecture. All this time we were training to be Officers and, in truth, there was a small but select group who took this very seriously, as, indeed, we all should. They took much satisfaction in being praised by the lecturers and were singularly unimpressed by those of us who relied on waffle to progress through the course. And although the more morally upright minority resisted the convivial distractions offered by women, pubs and clubs, I can appreciate that for some of us, the magnetic pull of algebra, calculus and advanced physics must have been irresistible.

As cadets, we were lowly paid and our finances were often stretched. I had never smoked but the other cadets were always cadging cigarettes from each other. Instead, I routinely chewed gum and, whenever I offered it around, there were always plenty of takers and the packet was often empty after I'd had only one or two pieces. I hit on a novel approach to this problem in the form of a laxative chewing gum, called Bonamint, which looked and tasted exactly the same as normal gum. I bought a packet of this and offered a piece to Jimmy, the Glaswegian friend from the original crowd, and as the class rolled slowly along over the next few hours he had a further three pieces and expressed his appreciation of both the gum and my generosity. It was only after the final piece of gum had been well and truly chewed that I advised him, and all the others, of the catch. We laughed but Jimmy just shrugged it off thinking I was winding him up. The truth dawned on him half way through 'Top of the Pops' that evening as he made a hasty dash for the toilet. Twenty minutes later he was off again on what would prove to be a busy night. It was Thursday night, disco night at Union Street and not to be missed, and Jimmy bravely decided to party on. I can still picture the scene clearly: Jimmy was slow dancing with an attractive, blonde nurse, obviously wowing her with his patter as he whispered delicately in her ear, then suddenly he pushed her out of the way and raced toward the toilets. As he flashed past me he shouted, "I'll fucking kill you, Moxley!" which seemed an extreme response to a friendly joke. Regardless, he received no sympathy from the others and whenever I proffered my chewing gum after that there were few takers.

I managed to bluff and cheat my way through all my exams without a care in the world at first, but then things started getting tricky. I suppose the first indication that I was stretching my luck was when I went for my Able Seaman certificate. I had done my normal preparation for the test, bugger all, even though I knew it would be a thorough examination of my knowledge of the theory and practice of seamanship, so I was relying heavily on my ability to waffle. On my way to the seamanship centre I bumped into a good friend, Moz, who was just returning after completing his exam. I felt sure he would have passed; he was a natural seaman and is still a ship's Master now, so I picked his brains. One of the questions in the exam concerned the weight of your last ship's anchor; I had no idea and asked Moz. When the examiner asked me the same question I gave the same answer that Moz had given to me. The examiner looked at me quizzically, then replied, "Oh, another one who's been on a supertanker, how did you find it?" Now, I had totally forgotten that Moz had just come off a supertanker, and I had never even set foot on one, so now it was time to more fully test the quality of my bullshit. Despite my obvious bias, I think it proved to be outstanding. By the time I finished I swear the examiner believed I had spent half my cadetship guiding helicopters in to land on the decks of these leviathans. Fortunately, I sailed through all my exams, including radar certificates, lifeboat man, fire fighting and watch keeping but, as they say, nothing good lasts forever.

I was burning the charred remnants of the proverbial candle at both ends, and probably in the middle as well. I have, over the years, developed an innate knack for getting myself into pickles and, as a rule, my pickles tend to be that wee bit deeper than most. If ever there was an example of the old line 'I'm always in the shit, it's only the depth that varies!" it is me. Without going into unnecessary details, the combination of too much of everything finally caught up with me and by the end of my second stint at college I was facing serious charges. A particularly exuberant night on the town celebrating the end of exams with Simon and others, culminated in an early morning dip in the pond outside the Civic Centre and then a chase by a pair of Her Majesty's finest through the back streets of Plymouth. The race appeared to have put the officers in a bad mood and, as I was the one deemed to have started it, they thought they would teach me a lesson. Rather than accept summary justice, I retaliated as best I could under the circumstances. Consequently, the wheels of justice began turning and I needed urgent legal advice. When the solicitor suggested there was a very strong prospect of a custodial sentence, assaulting a police officer was rarely eyed favourably by judges, I saw my fledgling career disappearing rapidly from view. My excuse was that there were two of them and I acted in self defence, which seemed to offer no real justification for my actions. His recommendation was that I should plead guilty and throw myself on the mercy of the court, and as I could not afford the services of a recognised silk, I was giving that advice serious consideration when I had a stroke of luck. Two days before I was due to appear in court I received a telephone call from the Chief Constable summoning me to his office. He asked for my side of the story before stating that in his opinion the case had been blown out of all proportion and, if I was prepared to plead guilty, I would be let off with a caution. Maybe he knew the story of Albert Bowes and didn't want to take any chances. Whatever the reason, I immediately agreed, breathed a grateful sigh of relief and flew off to Singapore to join another ship.

Life aboard the S.S. Hadriania was relatively peaceful, with leisurely runs ashore in South Africa and the opportunity to personally experience deep frying as we sweated for weeks in the Persian Gulf at the height of summer. We spent a couple of days in Dar es Salaam, the largest city in Tanzania, but I was far from impressed, it seemed to offer all the chaos of a city but with no redeeming features that I could see. Our next port of call was far more interesting.

Mtwara is on Tanzania's southern coast and lies in a huge lagoon, with an entrance that was so narrow we almost sailed straight past it. It was originally built by the British after the Second World War as part of their brilliant 'groundnut scheme', the aim of which was to supply industrial sized quantities of groundnuts to compensate for post-war food shortages. To implement this piece of genius, a railway line was constructed to accompany the development of the deep water port. Unfortunately, but perhaps not unforeseeably, the plan failed spectacularly and the railway line became defunct; the port, though still open, became underutilised and steadily fell into disrepair.

Mtwara town centre, Tanzania (Jim Shelley).

To its credit, the lagoon was stunning and it was a pleasure to head down to the beach after work for a relaxing swim. The town itself was as basic as it gets, but nonetheless pleasurable. One night I was making my way back to the ship after a few beers and decided to take a short cut through the long grass. I could see the dock in the distance and instead of following the road I turned off onto a well worn path leading straight to the dock gate. Halfway between the road and the ship I was brought to an abrupt halt by a lizard the size of a small dog, with a large, frilled collar framing its neck and standing stock still in front of me with its tongue darting in and out; the lighting was poor and it showed no fear whatsoever towards me, in fact, quite the opposite. I was tempted to throw something at it but felt this might make matters worse so, ever the hero, I ended up walking all the way back to the road; it was probably harmless but I didn't want to find out, and by the time I got back on board it was the size of a Komodo Dragon.

Mikandani Bay, Mtwara, Tanzania (Pepijn van Erp).

We left Africa and sailed for Bombay, now known as Mumbai. This was to be my first visit to India. 'Overwhelming' is a word that is often overused but as far as Bombay is concerned it is the only one that does the place justice. The sheer size and pace of this city is daunting, the discrepancy between the rich and poor is never more visible than here; the beggars with their twisted limbs are pitiful to behold, yet the wealth of others is so close they could reach out and touch it. The city teems with life: one minute you are staring in awe at the 'Gateway of India', a massive archway on the waterfront that reflects the local architectural styles and immediately takes your mind back to the

Colonial days of the British Raj, then in its shadow you could watch an old man with a millipede about nine inches long and an inch thick running in and out of his mouth and round his face, and just a few feet further along a snake charmer with a mongoose and cobra staging a mock battle, all this in the desperate hope of being thrown a rupee or two in their struggle to survive.

One day I found myself in an area called 'The Cages': it was like a zoo, but there were no animals in the cages only girls, many girls to each cage, and a bed in the back partially concealed by a curtain. It was not hard to decline their offers of pleasure even at the knock down prices. As with everything in life, all that glitters is not gold and a Scottish friend of mine who decided to take advantage of these apparent bargains came away with more than just a smile on his face, although he didn't know it at the time.

Next stop was Calcutta, now known as Kolkata for reasons I have yet to fathom; we berthed at a place called Buj Buj which is about fifteen miles down the Hooghly River from the town itself. The bus ride into town was an unforgettable experience but when we stepped off we were greeted with squalor the likes of which I had never imagined. It hit me instantly: people sleeping in gutters, beggars, noise, filth and a smell that hung oppressively in the heat. I am sure the place has a lot to recommend it but my overriding memory will always be of the squalor, poverty and the street kids who had to grow up immersed in it.

I was ashore with a fellow cadet, Smoothy Jack, and as we made our way through the streets we were besieged by shopkeepers trying to sell us their wares. "Johnny, you want sari? Leopard skin?" One managed to persuade us into the back of his shop and we had a cup of tea thrust upon us before we even knew what he was selling. As I looked around all I could see were rolls and rolls of material, and, as I can't sew, I had no idea why we were actually there. We were invited to sit down and then one of the men brought out a box from behind the counter and showed us its contents: it was full to the brim with bricks of hash. They had prepared a clay pipe of the stuff, wrapped a wet flannel around the stem to cool the smoke, and proffered it to me to take a puff. Now you need to bear in mind that up to this point in my life I had only taken a drag on a cigarette once and hated the taste, but it seemed rude to refuse and I didn't want to offend the guy after such a friendly approach. What harm could a quick toke or two do before we went on our way? Well, it didn't quite work out like that, instead I quickly found myself well off the planet, stoned out of my head and we ended up buying a brick of high grade hash.

We left the shop and went to the Officers Club for a swim and, as I was the one carrying the bag with our gear, it was only natural for me to put the brick in it. On the way back to the ship the realisation of what I was actually doing started to dawn on me and I began to feel increasingly uneasy. So I tucked the brick into the top, folded corner of my towel and rolled it up with my wet trunks before putting it back in the bag. As we approached the ship we counted about ten customs officers coming down the gangway and, as luck would have it, they stopped us and asked where we had been; one look in my eyes meant they knew exactly what I'd been up to. They got very excited and made a grab for my bag, which I indignantly insisted on opening myself, and holding the brick and my trunks firmly in one hand I let the wet towel roll down, explaining that it was patently obvious we had been swimming and what was all the hassle about. They calmed down and went on their way; I breathed a sigh of relief and could not believe my luck.

The next few weeks saw me and Smoothy making inroads into the brick on a daily basis, but it only affected my work once. I was on the four to eight watch with the Mate and he used to go down for a leisurely evening meal with the Captain about half past six leaving me to look after the bridge. I hated the smoking aspect of this malarkey and had decided to eat some, but had been advised that it would take a couple of hours to take effect. I thought that if I had some with a cup of coffee while the Mate was eating I would still be OK until I finished my watch. Wrong: by half past seven I was away with the fairies, giggling and sniggering with the uncontrollable hilarity that any and everything has under such circumstances. Fortunately, I still had the presence of mind to know that I had to get off the bridge. The Mate was back by then and I just buggered off and hid for a few hours and fabricated some outlandish excuse the following day.

It may sound improbable, but we bought the brick entirely on the spur of the moment and because it was so cheap. The thought of selling it on for a huge profit genuinely never entered our heads. We just thought it would last us for the rest of the trip and provide a means of passing the off duty hours. I know that would never stand up in court but it is the truth. A couple of months later we were on our way to Bandar Mashur in Iran and Smoothy and I had been informed we would be paying off there. By then I was so sick of the stuff that I threw what remained of my share over the side.

The day before we reached port I was called to the Captain's cabin for my report. As he was reading it out, it seemed so good that I honestly felt he must have picked up the wrong one; either that or he'd smoked some of my hash before he wrote it! The conclusion to the report was that I would be wasting my time doing another trip as a cadet and he recommended immediate promotion to Third Mate. I owed this entirely to the Mate, a certain Tom Wheating, who was one of the fairest men I ever had the pleasure to sail with. He had an infectious smile and you could not help but warm to him, he never abused his position and was quick to praise a job well done. We had a barber come aboard in Calcutta and Tom took the opportunity to get his hair cut. The finished article was a lumpy 1950's style short back and sides and when I laughed and pointed out that he looked like an overgrown schoolboy, he chased me round the deck to give me a hiding. I bumped into him about twenty years later in a pub on Dartmoor and he was absolutely convinced that it was me who had once put wacky baccy in the Captain's pipe, which only serves to prove the old adage: 'give a dog a bad name....'

The Captain paid off with Smoothy Jack and me and it was a

good job he did. After a sixty mile drive across a barren desert the ship's agent pulled up outside a pokey little hotel in Abadan and gestured toward the door. The Captain told him crisply that we were not staying in that shithole and to take us straight to the Abadan International Hotel; we nodded eagerly in agreement. In fact, I noticed that Smoothy seemed to be nodding rather a lot since we left the ship, and his usually tanned skin had paled despite the unrelenting desert sun. I had put it down to nerves and thought no more of it, though I began to wonder after he sheepishly distanced himself from an argument with an overly insistent porter who was determined to carry our cases. Much of the populace seemed to possess an uncanny ability to piss people off so we were glad to see the back of Abadan and apparently so were the locals, who all scarpered eight years later when the Iraqi army laid siege to it. Smoothy was particularly pleased to wave goodbye and I eventually discovered why: he was carrying what was left of his hash in his luggage, which perhaps explained his odd behaviour! I flew home to the prospect of enjoying some well-earned leave.

Think lightly of yourself and deeply of the world.
Miyamoto Musashi

6
At war

On my return to the UK I went straight to Plymouth to see my girlfriend; we were both quite young and as we had been dating for just a couple of months before I left, I was anxious about our relationship. We had a fantastic time and, with all the naiveté of those in love, decided to get engaged. As often seems the case when you are enjoying yourself, the time just flew by, and it came as a shock when the shipping company rang after just a couple of weeks to make me a very tempting offer: if I was prepared to go back to sea straight away they would promote me to Third Mate with immediate effect. Although I welcomed the dramatic increase in salary, I told them that I had no intention of cutting my leave short, I was not interested. It was my opinion that if I was considered good enough for promotion on merit then why should I be expected to sacrifice my leave; the two weren't connected.

While I was away at sea, my parents had bought a small newsagents shop in a picturesque Somerset village, so I took my fiancée for a quick trip to meet my family. It was while we were there that the shipping company rang again; they were obviously desperate to get me to go back and this time they had a carrot to offer: they said I would be flying out to Singapore as Third Mate to load a full cargo for Honolulu, Australia and New Zealand. Well, I had to think about it for a couple of seconds but there was no way I could refuse; after just four short weeks I was off on my travels again. I called into the shipping office in London to collect the ship's mail, a standard procedure, where I was dismayed to find that our destination had been a cruel deceit; it was a lie that would return to bite the company later. We were never sailing to Honolulu or Australia, but Da Nang and Nha

Trang, Vietnam; this was January 1973 and the war was still on but, on the plus side, at least we got double pay.

I arrived in Singapore to find the ship had already sailed and, as I couldn't join in Vietnam for obvious reasons, I had two weeks to kill awaiting its return. I was booked into the Cockpit Hotel along with a couple of cadets and it wasn't long before our wallets were empty. The ship's agent gave us a subsistence allowance, but whoever had calculated the figure must have lived a very frugal, reclusive existence as it was usually gone within a couple of days. The three of us were broke and sitting at the bar contemplating our options, such as meditation or chanting, when a hotel resident came to the counter, ordered a round of drinks, and nonchalantly told the barman to put it on his room. Eureka! Problem solved! And we had three rooms! I decided to be test pilot and casually ordered three Tiger beers followed by the magic words, "Stick it on my room, please!" while simultaneously waving my room key. It couldn't have been easier; now it was the turn of the other two. Once we had established that we all held the keys to a bright new future, the world was our oyster. Well, not exactly the world, the trick only worked within the confines of the hotel, but the hotel had various bars, restaurants and a fantastic nightclub for us to enjoy; which we duly did. This situation went on for the next three days until one afternoon, as we sat by the pool quietly minding our own business and indulging in some liquid refreshment, I noticed the ship's agent, Mr. Tan, striding purposefully across the garden with a look of anger on his face. There was no doubt about it, he was livid and blustered so much that at first I had difficulty understanding him. After a time I grasped the gist of his anxiety which was that, basically, he felt that we had been grossly irresponsible, let both him and the company down, and what we owed would be docked from our wages. Even my offer to buy him a beer was refused out of hand. As it happens the money was never docked from our wages so it worked out pretty well for us. Eventually, the ship returned and it was time to farewell the Cockpit and start earning our money. It came as quite a culture shock to walk out of our smart hotel and, half an hour later, find ourselves sweating on the deck of an old tanker; it took some time to fully readjust.

S.S. Anadara, 19,623t, Shell tanker, 1959-1978 (Kees Helder)

I was signed on as Third Mate and, as we pulled away from the jetty and out into the shipping lanes of the Singapore Straits, the full realisation that I was now an officer struck home in a chilling manner. I felt I had been promoted far beyond my capabilities and was about to be exposed in the most humiliating manner. When the Pilot had been escorted off the ship, the Captain, a dour Scotsman with a gentle disposition and a lifetime of experience ingrained in his face, turned to me and said the words I will never forget, "It's all yours, Third Mate, if you want me I'll be in the bar!" It was an instant laxative; I felt like putting my hand up and shouting out that there'd been a terrible mistake and it was all a bad joke. Of course, I didn't, I just did what everyone else did: got on with it and hoped for the best.

The Third Mate is responsible for keeping the eight to twelve watches, in the mornings and evenings, navigating while at sea, and loading and discharging cargo in port. He is also expected to 'shoot noon' at sea, which involves using the sextant when the sun is at its zenith to establish latitude, and to give the Mate a meal relief in the evenings. He is also responsible for the upkeep of the lifeboats, the flags, updating charts with new information on lights, anchoring the vessel and taking charge for'ard for berthing and leaving port. Nothing too complicated. To 'shoot stars', which means to use the stars to put a position on a chart, requires the use of a sextant to measure the angle between the horizon and the star. It is not excessively difficult but the measurement of the angle is critical and thus a clear horizon is essential. For this reason, star sights are always performed around dusk or just before dawn, which invariably falls on the Mate's watch. This explains why, on my first night on watch as Third Mate and still nervous as I entered the bridge to relieve the Mate, I was more than slightly taken aback when he asked me what I was like at shooting moonlight stars. I had never shot moonlight stars, I had never seen anybody else do it either and, more to the point, I had never even heard of it! Was he joking? Apparently not, as he explained that we were due to sail between a couple of shoals and it would help to confirm that we would be well clear of them. I tried to remain calm but I'm not sure how convincingly it came across, so I nodded knowingly and said I'd have a go; I wasn't really being given a choice. Well, when a sight of a star is taken it basically draws a line on the chart, and when you shoot five stars you thus have five lines and where they intersect is where you are. Of course, this presupposes they all cross in the same place; if they don't then it produces what is known as a cocked hat, and my cocked hat was so big I might just as well have stuck a pin in the chart for all the good it was. In the end, I just kept to the existing course, offered up a quick prayer and made sure I had a clear run for the lifeboat.

On the second or third night, as we were approaching Da Nang, I saw what appeared to be a ship on the radar but could not make visual contact. I asked the watchman to keep a good lookout but, despite the ship steadily closing, neither of us could see anything. The ghost ship was on my port bow and coming straight for us. In accordance with maritime law it was my duty to maintain my course and speed to allow the other vessel freedom to avoid a collision, which is all very well if the officer on the other vessel is awake, sober and aware of the situation but as he hadn't even switched on his navigating lights I was not overly confident that this was the case. I could now see the silhouette of a large ship and I should have sounded five short blasts on the ship's horn as a wakeup call, but this was only my second night in charge of a watch, and five short blasts usually means that half the ship's company rush out in panic and the Captain hits the bridge running, so there was a certain reluctance on my part to pursue this course of action. I bottled it, basically, and did the next best thing, put the wheel hard a-starb'd and went round in a great big circle finally ending up on the original course but with the other ship long gone. Well, that was the theory, but this was no ordinary ship, this was a warship of the U.S. Navy in a warzone, hence the blackout. They wanted to know what I was up to so he flashed me up and I tried to respond with our Aldis lamp but had only got half way through the word 'British' when the bulb fell out: part of the bayonet fitting had snapped off. I tried holding it in place with my finger but as it generates terrific heat that was a non starter; still cussing I tried to use the light on the 'Christmas tree' above the bridge but that had given up the ghost some years back. Hoping that the warship would sail silently away into the night, I just gave up, but the officer on the other ship was obviously not convinced of our innocence so came alongside, on a parallel course, and switched all his floodlights onto us; just what I needed. I only had time to flick him a friendly two-fingered salute before the Captain wandered onto the bridge and asked if it was bright enough for me; he then cracked a derisory joke about the Yanks and returned to the bar.

At the height of the American involvement in Vietnam, the port of Da Nang was the US Navy's largest overseas shore command, but by this time the Americans were trying hard to negotiate their way out of the morass they had got themselves into. In a last desperate attempt to bomb the North Vietnamese into submission they launched Operation Linebacker II, the most intensive bombing campaign of the entire war with over 100,000 bombs dropped on Hanoi and Haiphong. This, understandably, did not go down well with the North Vietnamese or the Viet Cong and I think it would be fair to say there was a high possibility of retaliation. Operation Linebacker II finished in December 1972, and three short weeks later the S.S. Anadara steamed majestically into Da Nang Bay carrying eighteen thousand tons of high octane aviation fuel. Needless to say, we discharged in short order and sailed down the coast to Nha Trang.

Shell had already had one ship mined and sunk at Nha Trang so we had every right to be concerned. The Americans could offer protection during daylight hours with a spotter plane overhead and, in addition, there was a small naval boat motoring around the ship throwing over the odd anti-personnel mine to discourage frogmen. However, this was not the case at night, so every evening as the light began to fade we would leave the berth and sail about ten miles out to sea and wait for morning before returning to carry on discharging the cargo.

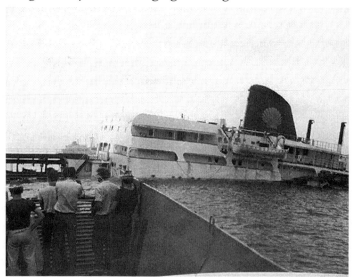

S.S. Amastra, mined, Nha Trang, 1967 (Barney Boylan).

I would stand on the bridge wing and watch the explosions ashore, I had no idea who was shelling who but there appeared to be a fair amount of activity. It was quite surreal and I felt like a spectator quietly observing someone else's war; it had been going on for years and we were just popping in to drop off a few supplies, nothing to do with us, so to speak. I subsequently read that the Paris Peace Accord was due to be finalised a couple of days later on January 27, 1973, and the terms of the accord clearly stated that each party would hold on to whatever territory they possessed at that time, hence all the activity.

Every night the small, local fishing boats would venture out, bobbing up and down in the darkness just a couple of hundred yards or so away from the ship. Sometimes they would get a bit too close for comfort but I didn't know how I could be expected to verify whether it was Viet Cong frogmen or a legitimate fisherman; we never covered this subject at college. The AB and I watched them like hawks but I could hardly call the Captain every time I had doubts as he'd have been permanently on the bridge, and there was no point in keeping a life jacket handy either: if we were mined a parachute would have been more practical! I was always relieved to hand over to the Second Mate at midnight but, in truth, I think he was none the wiser.

On our last day in Nha Trang we were preparing to leave and I was up for'ard raising the anchor. Everything was going smoothly when suddenly I noticed a fishing net was wrapped around the cable, and about fifty yards away a very animated Vietnamese fisherman was gesticulating frantically with his arms. I stopped hauling and advised the Captain of the situation and he suggested we give the fellow time to unwrap his nets as it was his livelihood at stake. This was highly commendable and I fully concurred with his assessment, however, there was one small matter for me to consider. As the officer on the bow of the ship I was dressed in full whites, tropical uniform, and the light was starting to fade. The crew was in normal work wear and blended in pretty well with the deck machinery while I, on the other hand, stood out like a big white pudding leaning over the bow. Of course, it was just my imagination playing tricks, but if it had been you the same thought may well have crossed your mind! Anyway, always calm in a crisis, I shouted down to the fisherman to pull his finger out, pronto; I have no idea what his reply was but he carried on unfazed as if he had all the time in the world. It would appear that I was not the only one getting paranoid, the sun sets quickly in the tropics and eventually the Captain gave the order to raise the anchor and cut the old sod's nets. The fisherman, understandably, had a few things to say about this but we had neither the time nor inclination to hear him out and he rapidly appreciated the fact that if he didn't start paddling as a matter of urgency he was going to lose his boat under the propeller as well. Two months later the Americans performed a similar manoeuvre and withdrew all their forces, leaving South Vietnam to their final inevitable fate.

We returned to Singapore to load a full cargo for Anchorage, Alaska and a new piece of navigational equipment, a Loran, came aboard. Because of the time of year, winter, and the distance to Alaska there was a high possibility we would face days without being able to get a sight, hence the Loran. It worked on reflected sky waves or some such and it was all a bit beyond me, but I made an effort to look like I was taking it all in; time would tell.

The Mate was newly promoted and had a very keen "in your face" style; not my cup of tea at all. He was built like an ox but on closer inspection you could see there was as much fat as muscle. He used intimidation with a certain degree of success, although his bluster was exposed the day he criticised the rope work of the wrong AB and ended up getting chased along the deck as the AB in question screamed at him, "I was tying knots while you were still taking marmalade sandwiches to school!" He informed me that we were stopping in Japan to load bunker fuel and he wanted an immediate inventory of everything needed to stock the lifeboats so we could have it delivered upon arrival. It was one of my responsibilities so I rushed through all the boats and came up with a list which included everything from pyrotechnics to barley sugar sweets. They were duly delivered in

Japan and, as I had to put them somewhere before I could distribute them to the relevant boats, the Second Mate said it would be OK to use his store locker. When I opened his locker I found brand new boxes of everything from pyrotechnics to barley sugar sweets that had obviously been ordered by my predecessor but not placed in the boats. That left me with a bit of a dilemma: either to admit my mistake to the Mate and get a right bollocking, not top of my wish list, or discreetly lose the lot and keep quiet: not a difficult decision. That night, after my watch, about half past midnight, I quietly slung the entire existing stock over the side into Tokyo Bay before returning to my bunk.

A couple of days out from Japan I went up for my evening watch and noticed the Mate had used the Loran to put a position on the chart, which obviously put me under some pressure to produce the goods myself, or look incompetent. Well, I played with this Loran thing for hours but could no more get a position out of it than I could get BBC news on it, which left me with a choice, be honest and admit defeat, or fudge it. It's times like this, on a pitch black night in the North Pacific, that instincts kick in, so I decided to fudge it. One way of getting a position on a chart is what they call 'Dead Reckoning', which means that as you know the direction you are steering and the approximate speed, and thus the distance you would have travelled, you just put a cross on the chart about where you think you should be. It is essentially a calculated guess as it fails to take into account variables such as the currents, the wind, your true speed over the land as opposed to your speed through the water, and for this reason you write DR next to the cross so anybody looking would know it is an estimated position. All I did was work out where we should be, but instead of putting DR I put 'Loran', the same as the Mate! Now, you can see where this sort of thing was heading. I handed over at midnight to the Second Mate who saw that both the Mate and I had managed to get a Loran position: what kind of Second Mate would he be if he couldn't get one? And so it went on, until the sun finally made an appearance over a week later and we got some sights and found we were miles, and I mean many, many miles, away from where we thought we were, but who was really to blame?

The officer of the watch always has a duty watchman with him. During daylight hours when the ship is at sea, the duty watchman is invariably employed in close proximity to the bridge so he is readily available should he be needed, usually to make the coffee. At night they pace the bridge wings keeping a lookout for ships, and make more coffee. These watchmen do a month on each watch and my new watchman was the AB who had dispatched a verbal broadside at the Mate only a few weeks previously; he didn't have a chip on his shoulder, it was more of a boulder, toward officers in general. He had thick, curly black hair, a broken nose and enough tattoos to raise an eyebrow, so it was with a slight air of trepidation that I climbed the steps up to the bridge for my evening watch that night. His name was Graham, and on the long, empty nights as we steamed across the North Pacific we spent hours in conversation, chatting about life, dreams and aspirations. I learned how he was a war baby, abandoned at birth by a mother who didn't want him and a father who didn't even know he existed, how life in the orphanage was all he knew before he went to sea. A bond developed between us that still exists to this day.

A few weeks later and we were sailing up the 200 mile long Cook Inlet on the final leg into Anchorage; the scenery was stunning, with snow-capped mountains on each side towering into the cold, crystal clear air. I stood on the bridge wing sipping coffee and taking in the view when, all of a sudden, I nearly choked on my drink; I could not believe what I was seeing. We were heading straight for the land at full speed. I ran across to the phone and urged the Captain to come up immediately, he obviously recognised the note of terror in my voice because he took the stairs two at a time and burst into the chartroom. He took one look out of the bridge window and rang 'stop engines'. It was an ice field. In winter, the sea freezes over and an ice breaker must clear a passage through; as you steam along, the ice floes part at the bow and reform together astern as you pass. I can't recall covering that at college, either.

Anchorage, although the largest city in Alaska, had the atmosphere of an old frontier town, wild and untamed; it nestles beneath the snow-capped Chugach Mountains, a huge range which dominates the horizon. It was almost surreal working the evening watch in port against this backdrop, I'd be on deck in a dirty boiler suit discharging the cargo while overhead the Northern Lights performed its magical dance like coloured curtains glowing and shimmering in the night sky.

The following day I went ashore with Graham and wandered along Fourth Avenue, the main street, which seemed to offer the best prospect of some excitement. The bars were decidedly rough and ready, the clientele even more so; the omens were good. After a few cold Buds we noticed that our bar had a tattooist out the back and Graham thought he might get one on his leg, which was about the only blank canvas left on his body, so I went in with him rather than chat with the ugly woman by the jukebox who kept winking at me. As usual, things didn't go according to plan, Graham decided not to bother and I thought it made perfect sense to slap a bluebird on the top of my right arm to match the shark on the other! I made a mental note to try and remember to get an inanimate object inked on next time around, before I started to resemble a menagerie.

I enjoyed a couple of good runs ashore before heading back to Singapore but it was the hurricane season and we ran straight through the middle of a giant. We had propeller problems and simply could not get out of the way of the mountainous seas and the howling wind. It was an unforgettable noise, like nothing I'd ever heard before. All we could do was ride out the massive swell as it tossed us about like a toy; it was akin to being on an out of control roller coaster and added a whole new dimension to meal times. The ship was battered so badly we had a week in Singapore undergoing repairs before loading another cargo for Alaska; hardly the Honolulu I had been led to expect.

It was on the return voyage to Anchorage that I started to give serious consideration to my future. I spent hour after hour

Fully laden in heavy weather.　　Hurricane damage (Dennis
　　　　　　　　　　　　　　　Hopkins).

alone out on the bridge wing, staring out into a wilderness of
ocean and not seeing another ship from one week to the next. I
had already decided that I did not want to pursue a career at sea;
it seemed such a waste of a life being cooped up aboard for
months on end and wishing your life away. I had no idea at all
what I wanted to do in the longer term, but I had an idea to
alleviate my immediate predicament. We duly discharged our
cargo in Alaska and had orders to sail to Trinidad, and it was
while we were en route that I hatched my little plan. I had been
lied to in an effort to get me aboard a few months previously so
it seemed perfectly acceptable for me to lie in order to get off. I
duly dispatched a telegram to the company saying I had domestic
troubles at home that required my immediate attention, and I
needed to return home as a matter of urgency. To their credit,
they arranged for me to pay off when we reached the West
Indies. There are those who might consider my action
disrespectful to the company but, as far as I am concerned, it is
all part of the game of life, and if the other party wants to cheat
then I'd be a sucker to play fair.

The voyage to Trinidad entailed a fifty mile passage through the Panama Canal, generally regarded as one of the finest feats of engineering in the world that enables shipping to traverse from the Pacific Ocean to the Atlantic Ocean without a lengthy detour round the notorious Cape Horn. The canal itself is a system of lakes, locks and channels that are an enduring testament to the tens of thousands of construction workers many of whom died, usually ravaged by malaria or yellow fever. It took about nine or ten hours to complete the journey and for much of that time I sat on the fo'c'sle head with a couple of the crew in the tropical humidity and heat and as we passed through one massive rock cutting a large bronze memorial plaque was clearly visible which paid tribute to their sacrifice. It was a sombre moment for reflection.

There was one last incident from that trip that still embarrasses me. I'd gone ashore with a colleague in Point Fortin, Trinidad, a small ramshackle village thrown up to serve the oil refinery. We were sitting in a bar enjoying a cold beer when a local approached us and enquired if we were the two men who had just come off the S.S. Anadara. We confirmed we were and he said that the refinery manager's daughter and her friend were over on holiday from Holland, they had seen us, were bored and, with nothing to do, wanted to meet up with us. Were we interested? We nodded eagerly and were soon in the back of a waiting taxi on our way to a very stylish beach resort. He instructed us to pay the taxi and wait while he established what was happening, and returned a couple of minutes later with a highly plausible line about the girls being tied up for a while but for us to get the drinks in; he even assured us that they would reimburse us. He asked for some money for the vodka and cokes and said he'd be back shortly; he'd only been gone a minute before the penny dropped, and, of course, we never saw him again! But credit where it's due, he was a first class con man, we'd not only paid for his taxi home but had settled his bar tab as well.

I paid off in Curaçao along with the two cadets who had joined ship with me in Singapore. We spent the first night celebrating in Happy Valley, and as we went into one of the bars in the compound we realised practically all the crew were there, boisterously knocking back the local rum. They insisted we join them and, as we didn't have to get back for our watch, it seemed like a good idea, a decision I came to regret as the night descended into a free for all. After consuming copious amounts of the powerful local rum, I stood up to find the toilets and strolled purposefully into a table full of Greek sailors, sending them and their drinks flying. They were understandably aggrieved and manhandled me roughly to the floor in full view of my ship's crew, a mixture of Scousers and Glaswegians who were well prepared for such occasions: no formal invitation was required to jump in and start swinging. One of the AB's who came to my rescue was Graham, he may have been short, but what he lacked in height he made up for in width, and his covering of tattoos and broken nose only served to enhance his image. When we met again in most unusual circumstances more than twenty five years later, it didn't take him long to remind me of my role in the brawl and how unbecoming it was of an Officer. We spent the next couple of days recovering by the pool before flying home: my life was about to take a dramatic turn.

Happy Valley, Curaçao (courtesy of ex-Shell tanker personnel)

Leave the wise to wrangle, and with me, the quarrel of the universe let be: And in some corner of the hubbub, couched, make game of that which makes as much of thee.

Omar Khayyam

7
Swallowing the anchor

I felt an unsettling mixture of emotions when I returned after months away. The elation at being back among friends and family was tempered by an uneasy suspicion that I was intruding on their daily routine, almost as a stranger. The fact is that I was living two quite separate lives, one aboard ship and another at home, and so were they, one when I was home and one when I was away. This often caused strained relationships and I had only been home a week or so when I had a row with my fiancée over something trivial, and before either party had the chance to understand why, I had packed my bag and caught the first train to London. I rang the shipping company and was on a flight to Singapore within days.

This was not unusual for me, acting in haste with little, if any, consideration of the consequences. By the time I had come to my senses I was thirty thousand feet above France and there was nothing I could do about it. I deeply regretted what I had done and my mind was in turmoil; I ordered a beer and tried to put on a brave face.

On arrival in Singapore I was pulled aside at the immigration desk and told to wait. I knew only too well what this meant, in the early 70's Singapore had a paranoia about long hair. It was not illegal but every public building, cinema and entertainment venue had posters declaring that any man with long hair would have to go to the back of the queue, and to describe what was considered long they kindly included a front and side profile of a face with the assertion that if hair reached your eyebrows or collar, or was over your ears, then acceptable standards had been breached. In anticipation, I had swept my hair to the side of my face and brushed it behind my ears, but the hair police were wise to my little subterfuge. As I stood waiting, thoroughly pissed off after a twelve hour flight, a long-haired Irishmen, Liam, joined my queue and asked if I knew what was happening. I told him he was about to be given two choices: either surrender his passport until he returned with short hair, most impractical under the circumstances, or allow the immigration officer to act as an impromptu hairdresser before being permitted to enter. He thought I was joking until we observed one of the officers had tumbled a hippy Australian wearing a wig; when the wig was removed his locks unfurled halfway to his backside. The officials were ecstatic with their new prize and quickly waved us through before setting about their victim with clippers and scissors! The irony was that although Singapore was desperate to clean up its image, and even banned chewing gum in the 90's, back in the 70's there were more Happy Houses, the colloquial name for brothels, than hotels, and drugs were easier to score than chewing gum.

Singapore, 1970's (courtesy of ex-Shell tanker personnel)

It transpired that Liam was a fourth engineer who was joining my ship. We had a couple of days in Singapore before flying on to the Philippines and, as he had never been further East than Putney, he wanted to visit the famous Bugis Street he had heard so much about. We had a few beers before arriving at the street in the early hours, just as it was in full swing, and had no sooner sat down than a Kytie and her friend sat at our table and said, "Hi Johnny, remember me?" "How could I ever forget you?" I replied without even a whiff of conviction. Liam asked how she knew me and I told him that here, all Englishmen were known as 'Johnny' but when she mentioned my shark tattoo which was not on view, it became obvious she remembered me from an incident in the past which slowly began to unfold in my memory. The previous year, I had been touring the clubs and bars before ending up in Bugis Street with Smoothy Jack and a couple of Scottish engineers when a pair of extremely hospitable Kyties attached themselves to our table as part of their normal routine to encourage sailors to pay for their services. If they happened to fancy you, they would go to great lengths to try and entice you to spend an evening of dalliance with them in their boudoir and as a fresh-faced eighteen year old, I became the focus of their attention. This was all part and parcel of life on Bugis Street and had never been a problem before; however, on this particular night the Kyties in question were in an extraordinarily festive mood and invited us all back to their place to continue the party. We were soon in a taxi and on our way, spurred on by the contents of many bottles of Tiger beer and encouraged by the Scottish engineers who, after four years at college, were keen to fully immerse themselves in the Singapore experience. We pulled up outside a building in Chinatown and I was led upstairs into one room while the other three lads behind me were quietly manoeuvred into the adjoining lounge. In my pissed state it took a couple of minutes to realise what was happening. Suddenly, I heard the lads shout through the door that they were heading back to town, and as I went to join them I was confronted by a locked door and both Kyties declaring their love for me. They were insistent that I stay and as I bent over to turn the door key one of them punched me hard on the side of the face. I may have been drunk but there was no way that was going unpunished, so I returned fire, opened the door and we all ran off laughing into the night.

'Who's a pretty girl?' Me & Kytie, Bugis Street, 1973.

Now, a year later, it would appear that the Kytie bore no grudge about the incident and we laughed it off. Liam loved the atmosphere and excitement of the place and didn't want the night to end. As daylight approached and the tables were cleared away ready for the morning traffic, he eagerly accepted the Kyties offer of a few more beers back at their place and coerced me into coming along. Despite my previous experience and against my better judgement, I joined them, which in hindsight was a foolish decision. Once in Chinatown we entered an old tenement block that had a warren of corridors and the Kyties had obviously prearranged to separate us, easily done under the circumstances and in my drunken state I was soon lost and alone with my old sparring partner. At the top of the stairs she exchanged a few words with a heavy-set Chinese minder who proceeded to give me a worrying stare, before she opened the door of a flat and led me in. As soon as the door was closed, she slapped me hard across the face and said, "This time you're mine!" which I found extremely unnerving, but was reluctant to fight back with the Karate Kid stationed outside. She took my shirt off and turned on the charm, but all that I could think about was how the hell I was going to get out in one piece. I quickly sobered up, asked her to get me a beer and as she went to the fridge in the other room I wrenched open the door in a flash, pushed the minder against the wall as hard as I could and ran hell for leather down the stairs and out into the street. This was in the days before Singapore had evolved into the ultra modern business centre that it is today, when large parts of the city were best avoided after dark; there were warrens of crumbling buildings housing an underclass of Chinese who eyed foreigners with suspicion. I found myself sprinting through the back alleys of the arse-end of nowhere searching frantically for a taxi. The next day, Liam and I joked about the events of the previous night but I couldn't believe I'd been so stupid and counted myself lucky to have escaped with only a thick lip and the loss of my shirt. Sadly, that night proved to be my last visit to Bugis Street and in the mid-1980's the whole place was redeveloped into a major complex of shopping malls and restaurants, thereby consigning a colourful and unique piece of sleaze and splendour to the memories of those who had visited in its heyday. A notable loss was the famous 'Dance of the Flaming Arseholes' performed on the roof of the street toilet by sailors and marines of Her Majesty's forces, with rolled up copies of the Straits Times burning brightly between clenched buttocks like incendiary flares as they whooped and hollered their way around the roof. It was a spectacular sound and light display, a prototype of the laser shows routinely staged at outdoor festivities many years later.

After a couple of full days we flew on to Manila which, in contrast to my previous visit, was now a city under martial law: there were soldiers everywhere and a curfew between midnight and 4am. We happened to be in a nightclub when the siren sounded and we were all locked in; not a problem from our perspective. At four in the morning, armed soldiers entered and we all quietly filed out and went home without any trouble. It certainly seemed to be an effective form of crowd control!

'Dance of the Flaming Arseholes', Singapore, early 1970's (courtesy of ex-Shell tanker personnel)

I had joined the ship in an optimistic frame of mind only to discover that the Captain was a tyrant who felt he could throw his weight around and treat the Navigating Officers with utter contempt; he and I fell out almost immediately and I gave him the full respect he deserved: sod all. He was well into his fifties, podgy, with wavy grey hair and a gait that was as close as you could get to mincing without actually skipping. He delighted in having, and abusing, power over others and there was ample evidence to suggest he was no stranger to the gin bottle. He would lose his temper over the most insignificant thing and there was not a Navigating Officer aboard who did not feel the wrath of his tongue for anything he perceived as an error. When it became obvious that an error was directly attributable to him there was never an apology, just a grunt before he stormed back to his cabin.

His sniping at me was continuous, there was never a day without his ranting abuse, and few, if any, of those rants went unanswered; he was determined to break me. On one occasion, I finished my watch in Singapore and handed over to the Second Mate; there was absolutely nothing to do aboard as the ship had to wait a couple of hours before loading and I was looking forward to a cold beer and a swim at the Officers Club. The Second Mate then informed me of the Captain's instruction for me to stay aboard and help him; he was clearly embarrassed to be put in this position as my help was simply not needed. I went straight up to the Captain's cabin to seek some justification for his action only to be met with a withering stare and a dismissive retort that he did not have to give any explanation, I had no choice, I must follow his orders. This was pretty much the answer I was expecting; I calmly told him that I was going ashore and the only way he was going to stop me would be to stand on the gangway, which, I pointed out, would not be advisable. I had a relaxing swim at the club and a couple of cold beers before going back for round two.

A few days later we were off Borneo and I was looking at an island through the binoculars when he came onto the bridge and asked what I was doing. When I told him he shot straight back, "That's not an island! It's a bloody ship!" "Well, if it is" I said, "It's carrying a cargo of bloody trees!" It was a never ending battle.

Another example of his tantrums occurred in New Caledonia, a beautiful island in the South Pacific. The ship was alongside in the port of Noumea, but the town was nothing like I imagined it might be. The place was wholly 'Westernised' and extremely expensive, and although we were told there were some beautiful beaches further along the coast, we had neither the time nor the inclination to go exploring. It comes as no surprise to me to find that it has never become a major tourist destination unlike the other islands of the archipelago. The run ashore was disappointing and I headed back to the ship for my watch but arrived ten minutes late through circumstances totally out of my control. The Captain happened to be strutting about on deck and noticing my late appearance, launched into a tirade in front of the crew, cadets and other officers. I completely ignored him and carried on tying up my laces which only exacerbated his frenzy. When he threatened to make sure I never got another ship and I cheekily retorted that I couldn't wait to get off this one and the last thing I wanted was another, he went ballistic. He was apoplectic, and I honestly thought he might have a heart attack. He could not believe that I was treating him with such disrespect and he was at a loss to know what to do. The anger in him was plain for all to see, he had been humiliated in front of everybody. He clenched his fist and went to raise it at me: he was in his late fifties and overweight, I was nineteen, fit and more than capable; all I needed was an excuse. He could see I was not going to be intimidated and, eventually, he stomped off to his cabin threatening repercussions.

On another occasion we were off northern Australia when the Radio Officer picked up an S.O.S. from a coaster called the 'Green Seal' that had sunk on its way back from New Guinea. The Australian Air Force was coordinating a search and rescue for the survivors and we were asked to perform a square search on some given coordinates in an effort to find them. I took over the watch that evening and the cadet, the watchman and I stared intently into the darkness in the vain hope of seeing something while we sipped our coffee. Almost miraculously, after about an hour or so we saw a red flare off the starboard bow, so I altered course and immediately rang down to the Captain. After some shenanigans with the lifeboat we finally got the three Aussies aboard and were hailed as heroes by the local media. I can still picture the Captain speaking to the local radio station about how he spotted the flare from the bridge and ordered the rescue; in his dreams, maybe. After the rescue, it was decided that it would be too expensive to divert the ship to put the Aussies ashore so we had to take them to our next port of call, Borneo. On the ship there is an honesty bar: you sign for your drinks and pay the bill at the end of each month, but, of course, the Aussies had no such account. The Captain was so pleased at his new found fame that he told the Aussies they were welcome to drink at the bar and to just sign the book as 'Green Seal'; he would settle the account. As luck would have it, I was standing nearby and happened to overhear and felt it could prove useful. I had never been in the habit of drinking on board ship before but this Captain was enough to drive a Muslim cleric to the bottle. Liam, who did the same watch but in the engine room, and I would meet in the bar after our evening shift and enjoy a few cans, which had not escaped the Captain's attention and he had found it necessary to have words with us regarding the quantities we were imbibing. The old maxim about the pot calling the kettle black could not have been nearer the mark! The good Captain had unwittingly provided us with the ideal solution; we carried on drinking as usual but, for the next week or so, just signed the bar book 'Green Seal'. I found it hard to keep a straight face when I overheard the Captain saying to the Chief Engineer, "Blimey, those Aussies don't half drink a lot!" They were sorely missed after they were put ashore, drinking our fill at the Captain's expense made the beer taste even sweeter!

Yet another incident where he decided to exercise his authority also backfired on him as we sailed through the islands of the Philippines. I'd had one can of beer before going up at eight in the evening to take over my watch. The bridge was in darkness and as I entered from the bridge wing I stopped to have a brief chat with the cadet on duty, Glen, a friend from college. As we were talking I accidentally burped, not the height of etiquette but hardly a hanging offence. Little did I know that Captain Fantastic was in the chartroom behind the bridge, talking with the Mate, and had heard my stomach erupt. He strutted onto the bridge, accused me of being drunk and threw me off. I calmly explained that if he wished to enquire of anybody in the bar he would be told that I had consumed just a single, small can of beer over the previous hour. He didn't want to know and made great show of throwing me off; I couldn't believe the extent of his pompous, crass stupidity but he wouldn't listen, so I left. Two questions remained unanswered: what was I going to do now, and, who was going to do my watch? The first question was easily resolved: I went to the bar. But the second question was proving more of a problem for the Captain: the Mate had just done a four hour stint and would be up again at four in the morning so he didn't want to do it, the Second Mate was due on at midnight so he didn't want to do it, which left only the Captain, and he sure as hell didn't want to do it. I was sitting in the bar enjoying a beer and contemplating my next career move when the phone rang; five minutes later I was back on the bridge and Captain Fantastic was back in his cabin, no doubt plotting my downfall! When I say I was enjoying a beer, that is not strictly true, it was very difficult to enjoy anything with that Captain aboard. Although I'm pretty easy going and don't worry unduly about things, the constant, daily sniping was getting me down, there was no prospect in sight of any letup and when the Captain was patently wrong there was never even a hint of acknowledgement of fault, never mind apology. Life aboard does not compare with life ashore; if a boss ashore is giving you a bad time you only have to put up with it until five and then you can go home and forget about it for a while. Not so on a ship where he can turn up in your cabin at any time, he's in the saloon when you go for your meals, he can turn up in the bar if you go for a drink, seven days a week, and for months on end!

One classic example of his ignorance occurred in the Sulu Sea when he wandered onto the bridge about eleven, looked at the chart, and saw lines drawn on it at regular intervals. Normally on the morning watch it was my responsibility to take sun sights and draw lines on the chart so we could ascertain our position at noon, but these were not sight lines. He asked me what they were and I replied that they were position lines taken from Mount Balabac, a much more accurate and, of course, easier option than taking a sight. Without even venturing out onto the bridge he shouted, "Don't be a fool, there's no way you can see Balabac from here!" This time I didn't waste any breath responding to him but merely walked out on to the bridge wing and pointed to the huge mountaintop in the distance before putting the kettle on for a coffee; he disappeared below without a word. This was typical of his behaviour. The company must have been well aware of this Captain and his reputation, but in those days they were desperate for officers, hence my rapid promotion; I doubt he'd last five minutes nowadays.

I paid off in the Philippines and my final report off that ship did not criticise my abilities but stated boldly that I had absolutely no respect for authority; I could hardly argue with that, for once the old sod had got something right! The ship's agent in Manila was most helpful: he could book me on a flight the next day or he would tell the company that there were no flights available and I could have the benefit of a few days there. I chose the second option in the belief that the company owed me a few days rest and relaxation for services rendered.

I flew home to an uncertain future. I had long since made peace with my fiancée but, as we had only spent a few weeks together over the previous year, only time would tell if the relationship could survive. Money was not a problem: the company owed me about three months leave plus another three months study leave, during which I was expected to cram for my Second Mates Ticket.

Having already established that I was not going back to sea there seemed little point in studying, however, the paid study leave was dependent on attending college, so I used to attend the first lecture, during which the register was taken, then quietly slip off when the tutors changed for the second class. Once out of college I was at a loss as to how to spend the day, but the local pubs seemed to offer a warm welcome and it was not long before I took up residency.

Until now, my alcohol consumption had been regulated by my work routine: I only drank to excess after paying off and during extended periods ashore. Aboard ship, I hardly touched a drop, and even during shore leave as Third Mate, I was well aware of my responsibilities to return and complete my watch. Now, with plenty of time on my hands, I spent the days drinking and the nights clubbing. It was 'The Seventies' and the era of 'Glam Rock' which meant we were dressed like clowns in loon pants and platform clogs, shuffling round ladies handbags on the dance floors and singing meaningful songs like 'Tiger Feet' and 'Ballroom Blitz', then staggering home with a box of fried chicken. I was back with my fiancée and had money in my pocket: life was good.

After six months I was out of money and out of a job, a situation which would become familiar over the following years but it was a new experience for me at that time. I managed to talk myself into a job as a mobile milk bar operator for the Milk Marketing Board. It seemed amazing to me that anybody would entrust this job to someone who had passed their driving test but never owned a car or driven more than a few miles. On the second day, they gave me the keys to a Landrover and told me to get used to it; on the fourth day, I had to drive up to London and pick up a twenty foot long, three ton milk bar and tow it back to Plymouth. I was an accident waiting to happen.

That summer I towed this contraption to all the County Shows, Air Days, Navy Days and Army Days in the West Country and, as luck would have it, one of the other milk bar operators had put me straight on how to make a good living at it. The trick was very simple and highly effective. The price list showed that flavoured milk was ten pence but a milkshake was fifteen pence, the difference being that a milkshake had ice cream in it and was whisked up to a frothy texture. The essence of this deception was that I would order a couple of gallons of ice cream so as not to arouse suspicion, and once that had been used up, to just go through the motions of scooping and adding ice cream before whisking the milk. Basically, I was selling flavoured milk, but charging for milkshakes, and raking in five pence on every one. When you consider it was perfectly normal to sell one hundred gallons or more each day at these shows you will appreciate that I had stumbled upon a lucrative little venture.

Despite all the mileage I was clocking up I had yet to master the finer points of towing, and one morning as I was on my way up to Aldershot Army Days, I plucked up enough courage to overtake a tractor on a dual carriageway. I thought I was doing fine until a sports car shot past me with two wheels on the central reservation. I was breathing an audible sigh of relief when there was an almighty bang in my rear. I pulled over and spotted a new Audi lying crumpled on the central reservation. Fortunately nobody was hurt, although the two in the Audi were understandably shaken. The police were called and took all the details and statements from witnesses; it appeared that my indicator wasn't working, and the prognosis didn't look good.

The police delivered an 'intended notice of prosecution' for dangerous driving and I became more than a little concerned about them delving too deeply into my past. I also recalled that when I had completed the original insurance form I failed to declare any previous endorsements, infringements or disqualifications, thereby invalidating the cover and leaving me open to yet another charge of driving without insurance! Things were getting messy, the show season was almost over, and I had an appointment in court for dangerous driving. I needed a plan. Two days before my court appearance, I climbed aboard a plane for Australia. I'd always wanted to see the place and now seemed like an ideal time.

And, as the cock crew, those who stood before the Tavern shouted. "Open then the door! You know how little while we have to stay, and, once departed, may return no more."
Omar Khayyam

8
Called to the Bar

It was a long flight to Perth, Western Australia, and to help pass the hours I took the opportunity to study Edward Fitzgerald's translation of the Rubaiyat of Omar Khayyam. Here was an erudite Persian mathematician and philosopher preaching the joys of a way of life that struck all the right chords with an impressionable young man like me: live life to the full, enjoy plenty of wine, women and song, don't worry about tomorrow or fret about yesterday. I may have oversimplified things somewhat but that was the main thrust of it and it certainly had its attractions as a template for life. I wondered what he would have made of the seafarers lot. I had expected plenty of wine, women and song, but to find it was mostly rum, bum and gramophone records came as a big disappointment.

I had no success finding employment in Perth so I took a coach to Sydney, a non-stop three and a half day journey. The landscape was vast, flat and empty, and hardly changed for mile after mile as it stretched to a distant horizon, and to make matters worse, much of the Nullabor Plain was rough gravel, bumpy and potholed, making a visit to the toilet a challenging and sometimes alarming experience. I chatted with a girl who was sat across the aisle, and it turned out she was a prostitute from Newcastle on her way to make a fortune selling her wares in the mining district of Mt Isa in Queensland. I flirted with the idea of asking if she accepted travellers cheques, but thought she might not see the funny side of it.

After arriving in Sydney I bought the morning paper and set

about trying to secure gainful employment. An appealing advert caught my eye, "Travel the golden triangle in public relations." Although not exactly clear about where the golden triangle was, the public relations bit sounded appealing, so I rang the number and within an hour or two I was being interviewed. It turned out to be peddling encyclopaedias door to door, a complete and utter con from start to finish, and two days later, I found myself fully trained and settling into a motel in Wollongong, a prosperous and sizeable port about fifty miles south of Sydney, with another lad and two girls.

There are only so many times you can be told to piss off before you start to consider that, maybe, this is not quite as easy as you were led to believe. Halfway through the first evening I turned a corner and saw a pub and, thinking a little sustenance was in order, I slipped in for a quick one which was followed by many more before the night was over. Unfortunately, the others in the motel, equally disheartened, were disappointed to have missed out, so the following day we all went. That pretty much set the pattern for our stay so, when the boss came down at the end of the week and saw that none of us had sold anything, he was far from happy; harsh words were spoken and the following day I was back on the job market.

I walked around a few of the hotels and bars in the town centre and fell on my feet in the Menzies Hotel. It was on top of Wynyard Street underground station, in the heart of the city, and had a complex of about twenty five bars throughout the hotel and station complex. I was employed as a 'bar useful' looking after three of the bars and learning the ropes. It was a walk in the park; it only took me about five minutes to establish that I could disappear whenever I wanted, as the bar staff just presumed I was in one of the other two bars I had to service. The hours were long but the pay was good, the beer was free and the rest of the crowd were brilliant. There was Mick, a Queenslander who was so laid back he was practically horizontal; Morry, a tall, slim Kiwi whose face was always grinning and his permanently bloodshot eyes betraying his favourite hobby, beer; Eric, the gay Indonesian illegal, and Susie, five feet two inches of pure, blue-eyed Aussie feminism. Mad, every one of them, which is exactly what they thought I was. Most nights after work we'd make our way up to Kings Cross, Sydney's answer to London's Soho, or go clubbing. Weekends were free and we'd all go to Bondi; life was good.

Despite all this revelry there was a bushfly in the ointment, and although I didn't appreciate it at the time, it would cast a dark shadow over a large part of my life for many years. Drink. Up until now my drinking, although the cause of many incidents, had not been a major cause for concern but now I was working in a bar the temptation was constant. Customers were coming in from ten in the morning, more than happy to buy me a beer in return for a friendly chat and a joke or two. The customers came and went about their daily business but as quickly as one customer left, another would arrive and the whole process would start again. By the time I finished at ten in the evening I was three parts to the wind and the night was still young. Looking back, I view my behaviour as boorish, but we were a young crowd with no responsibilities and just wanted to live life to the full. I worked with some of the best mates I'd known and we were so close that we seemed to encourage each other in every respect. We drank for free in each of the other's bars and our escapades got increasingly more daring, which inevitably meant that the next morning was spent trying to remember where we'd finished up and what we'd got up to, and, as often as not, it was better not to know. One incident that took some living down happened in the early hours in Kings Cross when I picked up an attractive girl I had been chatting to and, for no reason that I could figure out, threw her fully clothed into El Alamein fountain before wandering off. One worrying aspect of this was that I had no recollection at all of this until the others mentioned it and the events started to slowly come back to me.

Ironically, although my drinking was threatening to spiral out of control, this character flaw of totally carefree living and clubbing every night proved to be a magnet to others, who felt they were missing out on an enviable lifestyle. As a result, there was never a shortage of willing hands ready to join the party, and once the bandwagon gained a momentum of its own, it was not easy to stop; if you didn't feel like going on to a club there would be a chorus of encouragement from the others, to such an extent that it became an obligation. To further complicate matters, I had unwittingly become a well practiced and reasonably accomplished comedian. What started out as the odd joke often turned into a mini stand-up routine for a handful of locals which also became another source of drinking partners, as if I didn't have enough already. It actually reached a stage where I was offered the opportunity to do stand up routines in clubs but, to my eternal regret, I just didn't have the confidence or the courage: the fear of facing an audience was too great. I was to get numerous offers over the years but never found the nerve to accept any.

At least I still had enough sense to realise that this situation could not continue, and after about five months I knew I had to get out, I just could not keep up the pace. Heavy drinking was unavoidable in that environment and I needed a break. I got a job as a wool sampler for the Australian Wool Testing Authority, a grand title but really hard graft, or hard yakka in the local lingo. I had always pictured wool as a soft product so naturally figured that testing it would be a piece of cake. I did not know that when packed under pressure into 200 kg sacks it became hard, and I was expected to thrust a thirty inch steel tube into this solid lump a few hundred times a day. It was extremely physical as well as mind-blowingly boring; for the first few weeks my stomach was sore with the exertion but, eventually, I got used to it. The boredom was another thing altogether. The working conditions left much to be desired, it was a dusty old warehouse built in the late 1800's in the semi-derelict Pyrmont docks area; the building was so enormous I often felt as though I was alone in an abandoned aircraft hangar. On a more positive note, the warehouses were built to last and have since been converted into desirable waterfront flats.

As I was no longer working evenings I thought I'd try to get a part-time bar job to boost my income. At lunchtime over a quiet beer in a dockside pub called the Elephant and Castle, I enquired, on the off chance, if they needed bar staff. The landlord came out to ask if I had any experience and was duly impressed when I mentioned the Menzies Hotel. He then asked if I could handle myself and I told him that I'd done some boxing, spent a few years at sea and could look after myself. I imagined that, like most bars, they had the odd scrap and he just wanted somebody capable of jumping out from behind the bar to calm things down. He offered me a job, Friday and Saturday evenings, immediate start and fantastic money, and, as is the norm in many city pubs, white shirt and black bow tie was the dress code. I turned up the following Friday to be told, "You're on that door there." I tried not to look surprised and just nodded: I was a bouncer, it was no wonder the money was so good! It turns out this was the first pub in Sydney to have "sing-along", a sort of low-tech, early version of karaoke, in which somebody on a stage played piano, an overhead projector showed the words on a screen and the whole crowd sang along to 'Won't You Come Home Bill Bailey', 'Oh My Darling Clementine' and the like. The place would be absolutely packed.

The pub was on the corner of King Street and Sussex Street and had two entrances that were out of sight of each other. There were two bouncers on each door and nobody was allowed in wearing straight jeans or thongs (flip-flops), which just happened to be the national dress of the average Aussie male. Every ten minutes or so one bouncer from each door had to go in and collect glasses, so the other was left on his own. In Australia, most of the lads would drink in groups of five or six and you could bank on at least one failing the dress code. You can imagine the picture, half a dozen drunk, macho Aussies being told they could not join in the fun by a Pommy! I cannot recall a single night in the few months that I worked there when there were not at least a couple of scraps, and on more than one occasion there were so many patrons fighting that the melee spilled out onto the streets and blocked the roads.

On my first night there I was thrown straight into the deep

ocean and did not have time to ponder the situation, although I noticed that the other three bouncers all looked the part while I did not consider myself a particularly threatening figure. They were all larger than me with muscles and broken noses but not the steroid-fuelled, iron-pumping, mirror-kissers often seen modelling outside pubs today: they were fit, not inflated. The locals were eyeing me over, no doubt wondering whether I was a master of the art of kung fu or a Pommy with a death wish; in truth I was neither but the money was so good I didn't want to lose the job. Another major character flaw of mine is that I hate backing down from a challenge and, patently, the locals were aiming to test me out. It came to a head on my second night, the place was full to the rafters and I was inside collecting glasses; I had a column of glasses in my left arm and was picking up the empty ones with my right. As I approached a group of lads one of them held his glass out for me to collect and just as I was about to take it off him he smashed it on the floor at my feet! He was obviously emboldened after sinking numerous schooners of Tooheys and had decided to make me look a monkey, but unfortunately for him my adrenaline surged off the scale and the 'red mist' had descended. I dropped all the glasses from my left hand, grabbed him by the throat and delivered a few well aimed blows to his chin before depositing him outside on the pavement. While being the first to admit that this was probably not the most diplomatic way to handle the situation it did serve its purpose because after that the locals were far more accommodating. A few months later I left: I'd ridden my luck long enough and it was best to leave before I took an inevitable beating. The old docks have since been treated to a massive redevelopment and are now part of the stylish new shopping and entertainment area known as Darling Harbour; no doubt a welcome relief to the local police.

By this time I had left the wool stores and landed a job as a booking clerk with Pioneer Express, the main Australian national coach company at the time. After a few weeks they had a special assignment for me. Their main competitor was Greyhound coaches and they were anxious to know how many customers were travelling on their routes: they needed a spy. As the newest member of the team I was volunteered to go along to the Greyhound depot and count how many people were getting on and off each bus. I sat, sipping coffee, reading the paper while surreptitiously watching buses and counting passengers. They wanted me to do this every day for a week but by Tuesday most of the Greyhound staff seemed to be puzzling over whether I was suffering from a disturbance of the mind, had acquired an unusual fetish or worse, had developed some sort of rare perversion involving large passenger vehicles: I began to feel uncomfortable. The Solution: sit in a pub in Woolloomooloo for three hours a day for the rest of the week and just make up the numbers. The only real difficulty was trying to appear sober when I reported the results of this subterfuge back at the office. This comical scenario showed the tactics companies were prepared to pursue to beat their competitors. At that time, these were national companies with proud histories dating back to the 1920's and the competition between them was fierce. Few considered the possibility that one day these rivals would merge, then be taken over by another company to secure a monopoly on national coach travel in Australia, and the name 'Pioneer' would be relegated to the pages of history.

They were a good crowd in the office and I had a few laughs there. It was a busy place, open plan, and I worked in the 'express' section which dealt primarily with straightforward coach journeys, but there were other departments as well like 'tours' and 'accommodation' which are self explanatory. In the corner of the office was the telex operator who sat at her machine and typed away all day, and whenever I wanted a telex sent, a few times a day, I would wind her up by putting mine on top of the pile and ahead of everyone else's. There was always a bit of friendly banter and she was forever complaining because I never filled in the address section properly, mainly because the nature of the message meant the address was obvious. For example, the address was meant to consist of five letters, the first three were the town: PER was Perth, ADL was Adelaide, MEB was Melbourne and so on, and the last two letters were to identify which section, TR was Tours, AC was Accommodation, but the wording of the message, which was always short and to the point, made it perfectly clear which department it was meant for. If the message read, 'Book double room at Hilton 15/6/75 for Mr & Mrs Smith' then it hardly needed pointing out that it was destined for 'AC, Accommodation'. Of course, it would have been no trouble at all for me to put these last two letters in but by now it had become a means of injecting some spice into an otherwise mundane day. Anyway, one day I strolled across to the telex operator and promptly placed my message on top. I was halfway back to my desk when she shouted out, "EM EE BE what?" across the office, I turned round and it just came to me in a flash, I started singing, "EM EE BE it's because I'm a Londoner, that I love London town!"

I enjoyed it there and could have happily stayed on, but there was neither excitement nor mental stimulation and I felt in a rut. As once pointed out to me, the only difference between a rut and a grave is that a rut has no end to it. And with that in mind, I tendered my notice and decided to try my luck in Christchurch, New Zealand: The Land of the Long White Cloud, or as known by some: "The Land of the Long Lie Down".

Indeed the Idols I have loved so long, have done my credit in men's eyes much wrong; have drowned my honour in a shallow cup, and sold my reputation for a song.

Omar Khayyam

9
ENZED

Christchurch is the largest city on the south island of New Zealand; it resembled a quaint English town that had been stuck in a time warp for twenty years, and was so much more appealing for that very reason. It was hard not to fall in love with both the place and the people. I never seriously considered living in Auckland, a major city and the commercial centre of New Zealand; it always struck me as being a poor man's Sydney.

I managed to rent a flat in Champion Street, an ideal location being both peaceful and close to the centre of town, before turning my attention to job hunting. The local paper is always the favoured option and as there was only the one, my future career had to be lurking somewhere in its pages. There were numerous adverts for shepherds and farm hands, none for navigators, and two for bar staff. No contest: I rang enquiring after the bar vacancies. The first interviewer was as rough as a cattle dog and looked as if he was more inclined to drink his wares than sell them; when he asked if I had ever worked in a bar in New Zealand, despite me having told him it was only my second day in the country, I figured the relationship was never going to work. He asked me to ring him back but he sounded about as enthusiastic as me, so I didn't bother; his name was Les and our paths would cross again, only next time it would be me interviewing him.

Next interview was at the Hillsborough Tavern out on the Opawa Road with Mike and Peter. They were a friendly pair and the interview went well, but there was no offer of a job, just the standard line that they had other people to see and would I ring back next day. Could they not see what they were losing? Anyway, I had no time to dwell on temporary setbacks so headed straight back into town to pick up the afternoon paper and check out the vacancies. One particular advert caught my eye, it was the only one that did not involve shearing sheep or milking cows, 'Man in a million wanted'. Being the confident man that I was, I rang the number, and the very next day I was selling furniture at 'Cost Plus' in the suburb of Riccarton: the future had arrived! I could be opening my own store in a matter of months. Two days later I got home to find a note pushed through my letterbox, 'Ring Mike at the Hillsborough Tavern ASAP', and subsequently was informed that the job was mine and why had I not rung back? It pained me to advise Mike that I was now on my way to a glittering future in retail, but he suggested I come down for a drink and chat that Saturday evening regardless, they had a fantastic resident band and it would be a good night out. I duly arrived and was introduced to a host of convivial characters, all of whom insisted on buying me a beer. I was well on the road to euphoria at an early stage in proceedings, although not as pissed as the barman, whose place I would have been taking, and who some bright spark suggested I replace for the rest of the night. I felt it was the least I could do in return for their hospitality so I jumped in behind the Public Bar and the locals were so good humoured and supportive that by the end of the night I had agreed to give up my stuttering retail career and start work the following week.

It was a generous helping for a man to take: free beer every night, great bands and women everywhere, and it would have been criminally negligent not to enjoy it. But, though wine, women and song are a great basis for enjoying life, I savour a good argument and, in the absence of volunteers, I'm quite prepared to start one myself, usually with someone in authority; it was not long in coming.

After three weeks of unadulterated fun the owner, Robin, came down one Saturday night and invited the staff back to his house for a party. We were all into the bottle, me more than most, and after a few more bourbons I dived into his pool, naked of course, to sober up before delivering him a lengthy list of reasons why I believed he did not have a clue about running a successful pub. There was some truth in my tirade but I was out of order and it was an abuse of his hospitality, which I recognised only too well the following morning. Pubs were never open on Sundays so I had a day to stew over my performance and when I arrived at work on Monday I fully expected the sack. Mike, a tall, rugby playing Kiwi who looked like one of his ancestors had had more than a casual fling with a Maori, called me into the office and asked me if I wanted a drink. It was only about 10am, and I promptly told him I was sorry for being such a fool the other night and not to feel embarrassed about sacking me, I would save him the hassle and just leave, it was no big deal, I really was not unduly bothered. So it came as a total surprise when he replied that I had been promoted to Bar Manager; I was genuinely taken aback. I was offered an increase in pay and my duties were hardly demanding; I could not believe my good fortune.

As ever, life has a way of throwing you the odd challenge to keep you on your toes. Mine came early one afternoon on a beautiful summer's day when Gerry, the barman, came into the office and informed me we had a problem in the public bar, in the shape of a drunken patron who was Maori. The locals were playing 'king of the table' at pool, where the winner stays on and plays the next in line, often for a dollar a game, but he was king and wanted to play for ten dollars. I could see he was drinking a jug of ale so I took the requisite amount out of the till to reimburse him, walked up to him and, in a politely unthreatening manner, suggested that he was too good a player for anyone there, offered to refund his money for his drink, and asked him to leave. He told me he had no intention of leaving and what was I going to do about it? In general, Maori men tend to vary in size between large and huge, and he was no exception; he bore a striking resemblance to a brick outhouse with a similarly immoveable demeanour. My options seemed somewhat limited so I went to fetch Pete for support. I thought, wrongly as it turned out, that as an ex-policeman, Pete might have a novel idea on how to deal with the situation. Pete got the same response as I did so he advised the chap that he was left with no alternative other than to call the police, which seemed to displease the Maori considerably. Pete walked to the bar, closely followed by the Maori and me, and when he went behind the bar to ring the police, the Maori punched an old man, who must have been at least seventy, square on the jaw and sent him crashing to the floor in a heap. I was still not prepared to take this giant on face to face but stood over the fallen man to protect him from any further punishment, and with my back turned to the Maori, I suggested he leave quickly before the police arrived. His reply was a swift right hook to the side of my face and unfortunately for both of us that was a serious mistake; I just lost it and flew at him throwing punches. I landed at least three or four solid blows to his face before his arms clamped around my body and he lifted me clean off my feet, squeezing me like a python. I shouted out to the bar staff for help and both Gerry and Frank came flying to my aid: Gerry grabbed one arm, I was on the other, and Frank had his legs. We wrestled him to the ground but he was so strong he managed to keep lifting us up into the air as if we were lightweights, though he couldn't hold us there and every time his arms fell back to the floor I took the opportunity to give him a couple of hard right handers before grabbing hold in preparation for the next flight. After a while he began to tire, looking substantially the worse for wear, and a few other Maoris came over and said he'd had enough and told us to get off him. I was concerned that if we let him go he would beat the hell out of me, so there was a bit of reluctance on my part, but they assured me they would take care of him. We released our grip as they took hold of him and guided him out of the pub.

I breathed a sigh of relief, with one eye half closed. At least it was all over. Until, with an almighty crash, one of the huge, plate glass, pub windows smashed, and there stood the Hulk, stripped to the waist and bloodied, swearing to kill me! Oh shit! His mates got him back under control before one of them came rushing in demanding that I ring for an ambulance, apparently he had slashed his wrists when breaking the glass and blood was pouring out. I'm sorry to say I found it hard to show any level of concern and told him there was a public phone in the car park. Despite his protestations that the blood loss was so extreme he might die, I could not help feeling that he was being overly dramatic. Looking back, I feel ashamed to say that, at that particular moment in time, his demise did not seem such a bad outcome from my point of view. It is not something I am proud of but am not sure that, given the same scenario, I would act any differently now. Even as he was being carried away on a stretcher he was shouting "I'll kill you, Pommy Bastard!" and apparently he bore no grudge against the other two, which felt disconcerting if not racist.

The police came in and took statements before following the ambulance. The old man, Jack, was back on his feet and a couple of free tots lifted his spirits no end, in fact I think he secretly loved all the attention he was receiving. We got the glass cleared away and glaziers quickly replaced the broken pane, but behind all my bravado and joking I had a feeling that this may not be the end of the story.

That night, when Mike came in, he could see I was quieter than usual and asked why. I explained my concern that, when the Incredible Hulk got out of hospital, he knew where I worked and could pick his time to take revenge. Mike suggested that by the time he got out of hospital, after having had such a beating and possibly losing the full use of his hands, the last thing he would want would be more of the same. I was not totally convinced but it made sense and eventually proved to be the case.

One thing this fracas brought home to me was the consistency of human nature; lust, jealousy, greed and violence are part and parcel of life everywhere, although in some parts of the world the consequences can be easier to handle. For instance, in those days many Indian, Chinese or Malay people were physically smaller than me, a definite advantage in a conflict situation. Many Polynesians, on the other hand, are quite the opposite, think Jonah Lomu, and are famous for their strong warrior culture. The All Blacks rugby team even perform their legendary Haka, a war dance with overtones of throat slitting, at friendly games, so you can appreciate the potential pitfalls facing the unwary, something Captain Cook may have missed. Add alcohol to the mix and the effect can be reminiscent of fuel on a bonfire.

A few weeks later the assistant manager absconded with ten thousand dollars from the pub safe; he was a heavy gambler and had got himself into debt with the wrong kind of people. He was almost immediately arrested at a race track in Auckland and finished up in jail; I ended up with his job. I did miss him, he was a larger than life character and there are far too few of them about. He had a presence that could genuinely light up a room the moment he walked in. Unfortunately, he also had drinking and gambling problems that he struggled to overcome. I got a letter from him many years later saying how he recognised his demons and was determined to overcome them, and to that end, he had purchased what he was convinced was going to be a champion greyhound. You had to admire his style.

I welcomed my promotion to assistant manager, the extra money came in handy and the bar was easy enough to run. We had a band on every night, except Monday and Tuesday, and a good one on Saturday afternoons as well. As is usual when alcohol is consumed in large quantities, violence was never far away. I would try to talk people round before the bouncers were called upon but it didn't always work and fights were a common occurrence. The police advised us that, in their opinion, bouncers often provoked the violence and suggested we try a period without any. I was not entirely happy with this but the owner decided to give it a try, although with the benefit of hindsight, such experimentation a week or two before Christmas had its weaknesses. On Christmas Eve the place was packed and we seemed to have avoided any trouble, so at closing time I locked the tills in the Public Bar and Off Licence, and strolled to the Lounge only to find the majority of the customers standing on their tables and chairs, barracking their support loudly and looking toward the dance floor at the far end of the building. I rushed through the crowd and as I neared the dance floor I was greeted by what is best described as a riot: thirty or forty people swinging wildly at each other. The group on stage was called Edge and their lead singer was a little guy called Denny who spotted me and shouted into the microphone, "John, do something!" Very inspiring but not especially helpful. I rushed straight into the office and rang the police, informed them that this was the Hillsborough Tavern, we needed rapid assistance, and could they send a few officers here as a matter of urgency? The operator politely informed me that it was the same situation at other hostelries and they would get there as soon as they could. I felt like pointing out that it was because of their daft advice to do away with bouncers that we were in the shit but decided it wouldn't help our cause.

By the time the officers arrived all the combatants had punched each other stupid and gone home; leaving us up to our ears in broken glass waiting for Santa. This taught me an important lesson to never rely on the police; they have their own priorities which are often some distance from the real world. A case in point was early one Saturday evening when we had a visit from half a dozen police officers who wandered casually among our customers, supposedly checking for underage drinkers. When I engaged one of them in conversation the truth came out: they were on their way to a dockside pub called 'The British', where a big fight was underway and had paused in transit at our pub in the hope that it would be all over by the time they arrived. I'm not sure the landlord of the hostelry in question would have appreciated that little joke. As I write these words thirty six years later the Tottenham riots are still fresh in people's minds, where the police stood back and let the mob trash and burn the streets of London, despite the desperate pleas of residents for help. Funny thing is, if you try to sort it out yourself you risk being called a vigilante!

Anyway, we had established that there was no way we were going to carry on without bouncers, so we took on a one man demolition expert called Kev. He was a tall, good looking fellow built like a boxer with a ready smile that hid his steely determination and supreme confidence in his undoubted talent for rendering people unconscious. He established his credentials on the first night in the most conclusive manner, at the expense of a trouble maker's nose. When I enquired if quite so much force was necessary, he nonchalantly replied that the culprit would never come back, which was true, he didn't! His reputation spread rapidly and the pub settled into a relatively peaceful period.

I clearly remember one incident shortly after his arrival, when we left the pub in the early hours and drove to a take-away. We were hardly subtle as Kev's three litre Oldsmobile thundered up to Cathedral Square in the centre of Christchurch, to eat our burgers. We had only just started our meal when a police car pulled up behind us and a young constable came over to question Kev, who proceeded to completely ignore him as he digested his late supper. When the constable called for backup a second officer arrived and they informed him they were going to arrest him. I was at a loss to understand what was happening, and presumed that the police could do what they said but it was clear that Kev had no intention of getting out of his car and sat calmly eating his burger. He duly turned to the young constable and advised him to get on the phone to the station and tell the station sergeant he was going to arrest Kev X. This he did, only to be told in the clearest terms, to just leave him alone, and off they went licking their wounds. I never understood at the time what the incident was about and am still none the wiser now, although I know that Kev had previously been jailed for a fight involving a policeman and this may have had some bearing on the situation.

Kev and I got on well over the next few months. He was a dangerous character with a variety of nefarious business interests of which I was well aware and I tried to distance myself. This wasn't always possible; sometimes just being in his company meant you overheard conversations which made you appreciate just how casual he was about the risks he was taking. One time a couple of likely looking lads met us in a car park and a substantial quantity of cash was exchanged for a package; I never asked what was in it but I'm guessing it wasn't jellybeans. Like most of his ilk, if they like you they can be good company. The last I heard of him he was running a nightclub in Kings Cross, Sydney, which would have provided an excellent outlet for his undoubted talents.

I took a week's holiday that summer, hired a van, stuck a mattress in the back, and my girlfriend and I headed over to the West Coast. The West Coast of the South Island was as far removed from Christchurch as you could imagine, it had a reputation as being the Wild West of New Zealand and the locals didn't disappoint. They had all the warmth of the average Kiwi but with none of the rough edges knocked off; they also had a capacity for alcohol which suggested the local publicans had few financial worries.

By early afternoon we were well into Arthur's Pass National Park, the highest pass crossing the Southern Alps, and pulled into a welcoming hostelry for a beer and a bite to eat. We finished one jug of ale but when I went up to order another and enquire about food, the barman directed us to another part of the hotel and suggested we get a move on as they would stop serving soon. We set off in the direction he'd indicated and when I spotted a host of people queuing for food I assumed it must be the restaurant so we joined the end of the line. The menu was written on a large blackboard above the servery, broiled chicken and various accompaniments, but there were no prices shown and I suspected it could be on the pricey side. There was nowhere else we could go so we filled our plates and as there was no till in sight, just assumed we would pay on the way out. We sat down and started eating. Hungry after the long drive, we were intent on devouring our meal but as I glanced around I noticed everybody else was smartly turned out, in contrast to our t-shirts and jeans, and no-one else was eating. It was when we heard the words, "Ladies and gentlemen, the bride and groom!" and everyone stood up, that I realised we had gatecrashed a wedding reception! We stood, clapped politely, finished our chicken and slipped out: we felt it best not to stay for dessert. Not a word or raised eyebrow was cast in our direction.

Next port of call was a pub on the outskirts of Greymouth, a coastal mining town. We arrived on Sunday and the pubs were shut, but one of the locals at the Hillsborough Tavern had told me to just go round the back, knock on the door, and shout, "Fred from Christchurch said to call!" Fred really was his name, this wasn't a code. The pub seemed well and truly closed but, despite my reservations, I thought I'd give it a go. A large Kiwi answered the door and no sooner had I mentioned Fred than we were ushered in with open arms, the place was in full swing and we could not have been made more welcome. A few hours later we staggered out into the darkness, drove the short distance to a nearby lake and parked up for the night. I woke up in the middle of the night with a raging thirst but nothing in the van to drink, the only option open to me was the lake, so I was forced to stumble naked through the undergrowth and down the bank to the water; my curses must have been heard for miles around.

We toured all over the South Island and the scenery in the Southern Alps was absolutely beautiful, a stunning vista of rugged, snow-capped peaks, dramatic glaciers, tranquil lakes and rivers of turquoise that coursed through the valleys like their lifeblood, it felt like another world. Although the mountain range stretches the entire length of the island, it is in the far south west that the most spectacular views can be found. Tarmac roads had not yet reached that far in the mid-70s and the rough gravel roads, single track in many places, lent a feeling of untamed isolation to the Haast and Lindis Passes and tested both the hire car's suspension and my backside on the trip down to Milford Sound. Picturesque Queenstown was at the centre of it all and was so reminiscent of a famous film set that I half expected Julie Andrews to stroll round a corner in full song. It is now on the backpackers trail and crowded with students taking a gap year; no doubt a boon for local businesses but I'm thankful I saw it before it became the bungee jumping centre of the universe.

Stunning Queenstown with Southern Alps behind (Jack Moxley).

Magnificent Milford Sound on a rare day (Jack Moxley).

As in Sydney, the strain of my lifestyle began to show after about nine months. Every night was Saturday night, all the staff were great and the locals were like old friends, but my liver suggested that it was time to move on. It was about this time that Mike decided to return to his car sales business and I was offered the position of manager. I declined and told him of my intention to leave, but agreed to stay on until Mike's replacement had learned how the operation ran. One of the applicants was the manager of the very first pub where I applied for work when I arrived in New Zealand. I was tempted to give him a hard time but he was OK, he had shed his cattle dog image and we ended up getting on well.

I was sad to leave but my plan was to join a homeward bound ship and work my way back to the UK. Having completed my usual amount of research i.e. none, it should have come as no surprise when I discovered that union rules meant this was not as easy as I had envisaged and, as a result, within three weeks I was broke and out of work, again. I rapidly secured a job in a local iron foundry; it was back breaking, filthy work. I started at eight in the morning when the moulds of burnt sand that had been used overnight were put onto a conveyor belt and carried to the top of a large hopper into which they were deposited for reuse. My task was to sit atop this hopper in a cloud of fine dust, and ensure the sand was evenly distributed: by nine in the morning I looked like Sammy Davis Junior. Suitably blackened, I spent the rest of the day breaking scrap iron into chunks sufficiently small to fit into the blast furnace for the afternoon smelt. As jobs go, this one did not have a single redeeming feature. So I picked up my wages on Friday and by Saturday afternoon I was relaxing on a plane high above the Tasman Sea, with a cold Steinlager close to hand. If my dire financial predicament necessitated such menial work then I might as well do it in Australia where they at least pay you well for the humiliation.

I left New Zealand with nothing but the fondest memories and a desire to return one day. I am still in contact with Mike, although my dream of meeting up with him for a jug of beer at the Hillsborough Tavern was shattered when the pub burned down in 2009 and was subsequently demolished: as a result of a misunderstanding, it hadn't been insured!

Indeed, repentance oft before I swore – but was I sober when I swore? And then came spring, with rose in hand, my threadbare penitence to pieces tore.

Omar Khayyam

10
The deep north

As I walked across the tarmac to the airport terminal I heard my name being called and looked up to see a few old friends, who I had told of my return, prophetically shaking a can of beer and spraying it over the viewing platform. I only stayed a couple of days in Sydney before heading for North Queensland. Five of us squeezed into Mick's clapped out Holden car and set off on the 1400 mile trip. At the time, I had no idea that I was retracing the footsteps of one of my ancestors. The London branch of the Moxley family have a tradition of calling the eldest son Sylvanus, a practice carried on by my father and a much used source of mirth and piss-taking in my youth. One advantage of this moniker is that it greatly assists in tracing the family tree and as a result, I established that Thomas Crowley Moxley had forged the trail way back in the 1800's. The London census of 1861 records him as a resident of Shoreditch who was employed as a Steward in the Merchant Service. It transpired that he jumped ship in Australia and married a local girl in 1863, then proceeded to father twelve children and become the first Licensee of The Great Western Hotel in Woody Point, Brisbane, now known as The Filmers Palace Hotel. His father was called Sylvanus, as was his son, and in true Moxley fashion he was eventually charged with fraudulent insolvency. Thomas' legacy to his adopted country did not end there as the available evidence suggests that his grandson, William Cyril Moxley, better known to the police as Mad Dog Moxley, was hanged at Sydney's Long Bay Gaol in 1932 for the brutal double murder of a young woman and her boyfriend. His father was Walter Sylvanus Moxley and he was one of the last men to be executed in NSW, which may go some way towards explaining why I had so much trouble getting through immigration at the airport.

We stopped at the Gold Coast, roughly half way, to consider our options and it was there that one of the lads decided to return to Sydney; the rest of us carried on to Mackay where Mick had managed to line up a job for himself. After a day in Mackay, another lad felt he'd done enough travelling and headed back to Sydney, which left just my girlfriend, Kim, and I standing by the highway trying to hitch a ride north. We reached Bowen, a small, busy port, where we were assured that we would soon be earning a fortune picking tomatoes, but the tomatoes had plans of their own and had delayed ripening indefinitely. We found a small guesthouse and I spent most days jogging out to Kings beach and swimming in an effort to regain some fitness in preparation for the long overdue harvest. Lunchtime invariably consisted of the cheapest item on the menu, steak, washed down with copious ice cold XXXX followed by a game or two of pool. It was during a pool game that a helpful local enlightened us about the deadly box jellyfish and pointed out that the beach wasn't netted and sharks were common, which went some way to explaining why I was the only one ever taking advantage of the warm water for swimming. Our patience finally ran out after nearly two weeks waiting for the reluctant tomatoes, and we decided to move north again in search of work.

We eventually arrived in the small township of Home Hill, went into the pub and asked if there was any work about, and were advised that a plantation owner a few miles out in the bush was looking for a labourer. I left Kim in the pub and started walking; after about three miles I saw an old man sitting on his doorstep and thought it might be a good idea to check if I was heading in the right direction. "Who wants to know?" he asked and I replied that I'd heard a plantation owner was looking for a worker and I was looking for work. "Can you drive a truck?" he enquired and, thinking it couldn't be that difficult, I assured him

I could. He seemed impressed with me and promptly offered me a job and a place to live.

It was a big wooden shack on stilts, sitting in the middle of a large clearing and surrounded on all sides by tall sugar cane. There were fruit trees aplenty with mangoes, oranges and bananas all within easy reach, and a patch of beautiful, shiny aubergines. Water was pumped up from an underground spring by a windmill type contraption and, if you wanted hot water, the pipe was diverted through a couple of coils inside a mud oven, you just threw in a few bits of scrub wood, lit them, and there was your hot water and shower. Very basic but most effective, and I wouldn't have changed it for the world; for a city boy born and bred this was like the adventures of the Swiss Family Robinson. It was mine until his regular driver returned for the cane cutting season in a few weeks, but I was more than happy with that arrangement.

I was put to work clearing scrub from the drainage channels to the river and general labouring. It was so hot and humid that on one particularly oppressive day I thought I'd have a dip in the river to cool down but, as I edged along a tree branch to get a clear drop into the water, I must have disturbed a snake, which promptly slithered into the river just ahead of where I stood; I decided to let the snake enjoy a quiet swim alone.

I spent a few days planting sugar, which I had imagined would be an easy job, dig a small hole, drop in a few seeds and move along, but my idea was way off the mark. Planting involved hand feeding seven foot lengths of cane into a cutter attached to the back of a tractor while simultaneously balancing on a thin platform on the side of the trailer, as it endlessly bounced up and down in the dried mud furrows for hour after hour in humid 90F/30C heat. By the time we finished the first day, my hands were red raw from manhandling the rough cane and I was physically exhausted from trying to keep my balance on the trailer. It was a hard day's work, as tough as I had ever done, before or since.

When I finally got back to the house, sore, knackered and

hungry, I found Kim in tears and no tea ready, not the welcome return I had hoped for. It turned out that the cause of all the distress, and subsequent lack of any tea, was a snake curled up between the oven and the wall, level with the cooking rings and flicking its tongue out every two seconds. I was not in a mood to compromise, we were miles from anywhere and the light was fading. Despite having heard all about the deadly taipan, my stomach insisted that this thing had to go. I tried teasing it out with a spade but it was an awkward bugger and was clearly getting angry; so was I and I ended up cutting its head off before switching on the cooker rings. It turned out to be a harmless tree snake that had got in via the orange tree, but when anything gets between me and food there's no such thing as harmless.

After tea I went out for a shower that always had to be shared with half a dozen or more cane toads. These poisonous toads are everywhere; they were first released en masse into Queensland from Puerto Rico back in 1936, in the hope that they would emulate their success at home by eating the beetles that were threatening the sugar plantations of Australia. The plan seemed perfectly straightforward but, as is so often the case, proved to be spectacularly unsuccessful; the cane fields could not offer sufficient shelter for them so the toads left the beetles alone and proceeded to eat or poison the local wildlife instead. The females are very large, they average about five or six inches long in the body, and weigh in the region of a couple of pounds, and to top it all, they are just so damn ugly. There is some irony in the fact that the Australian Government decided to ban the import of German shepherd dogs, an established and proven worker, shortly before they approved the release of the cane toads to wreak havoc on the natural flora and fauna. It was an unfortunate decision that has continued to resonate more than 70 years later.

As my time on the plantation approached the end I began looking for another job. One Saturday morning I walked into Inkerman sugar mill on the edge of town, saw a few guys having their coffee break and asked if there was any work to be had:

bingo! I got lucky. I started the following week and even found a rundown flat in town to rent.

Home Hill sugar mill and cane train (Bill Strong).

For my first week's work at the mill I stayed in the cane field shack and walked the three miles into work. Early one morning I noticed a giant Red Kangaroo on the other side of the road taking altogether too much interest in me. I presumed it was somebody's pet as it had a collar on, but it was hopping along looking very intimidating. These powerful creatures are about six feet tall, and when it started to cross the road I was more than a little alarmed. I threw a large stone at it and, much to my relief, it got the message and turned back.

Working at the mill was great, the whole building was being modernised and expanded and I was working with a sub-contractor who had a fair number of jobs to complete. We worked seven days a week and I was earning incredible money, and as I was meant to be self employed, I wasn't paying any tax either. Sometimes after work, a few of us would go down to the Burdekin River which ran alongside the site, and as it was the dry season there were sand dunes standing proud in the water on which we'd set up an improvised barbecue to cook our steaks while the beers were chilling in the river. We'd swim, get drunk and chat about everything and nothing in particular: it was perfect. I found out about the resident crocodiles some time later.

Burdekin River meandering peacefully in the dry season (Bill Strong).

One day a neighbour and friend of mine invited me to go duck shooting of an evening with him and his mates. I'd never fired a rifle before but it seemed like a good idea so I turned up at the appointed pub and off we went. We all crammed into a couple of open top Holdens that everybody seemed to have in the bush and drove to a deserted rice field. At first I thought I must have misheard them; it surprised me to learn that they actually had rice fields in the Burdekin area. The other lads were real characters who bore an amazing resemblance to the cast of the Walkabout pub in Crocodile Dundee, Donk in particular springs to mind. The chap who seemed to be in charge issued a brief instruction to the effect that if any strangers turned up we should all jump into the motors and make a hasty exit; this was deemed necessary for the simple reason that it was out of season for duck shooting: rather an inopportune time to be told, I felt! Anyway, we took up position and waited for the ducks, and waited, and while we waited the mosquitoes came to bite; the Aussies seemed immune to their bites so I suffered in silence rather than enhance the image of the notorious Whingeing Pom! Eventually, we saw birds silhouetted against the night sky, shots rang out and we ran in excited expectation across the field only to be confronted by the unmistakeable and lifeless body of a Black Swan, one of the national icons of Australia and a protected species to boot, laying pitifully in the rice: "Strewth, let's piss off to the pub!" voiced one of the locals, and there was all round agreement.

One of our jobs at the mill was servicing the conveyor belt carrying the fresh brown sugar straight out of the machines, still warm and fragrant like honey; I could not resist scooping it up and taking the odd mouthful. The whole atmosphere on the site was laid back, nobody was worked to death: the union made sure of that. Some wag had even written on the back of one of the toilet doors, 'Gone to work, back in ten minutes!'

Home Hill had little attraction for visitors. It was a small unremarkable township that existed in the shadow of Ayr, a few miles north across the huge Burdekin bridge, but the only appealing thing about Ayr was that it had six pubs instead of three when we fancied a change of venue; they didn't even have a decent beach between them and for a pair of coastal towns that's quite an achievement. The most unforgettable sight in the area was the burning of the sugar cane. The night before it was cut and transported by the miniature railway network to the mill, the leaves had to be burned off the cane. This was obviously done in a controlled manner with the necessary fire breaks but, from a distance, it looked as though the whole horizon was in flames: spectacular.

The rest of the gang were a pleasure to work with. We'd take the odd day off work and go out to the islands, hire a boat or a mini-moke and generally have fun, but after a few months I felt it was time to move on again. I rang Mick in Mackay and told him I

Burning the cane prior to harvest (Rob & Stephanie Levy).

was earning a fortune so he came up and took over my job and my flat. He brought his black Labrador, Ben, which was interesting because the resident mutts had a lifestyle quite unlike back home. There was a pack of about half a dozen dogs that, despite having owners and being well cared for, had a level of freedom to roam which would be considered irresponsible in a city. The undoubted leader of this pack was Schultz, a German short haired pointer who was the smartest hound I have ever encountered. He would never go inside any building other than one of the three pubs in town; I couldn't even tempt him in with a juicy piece of steak. I would often walk to the shops and he'd happily fall in behind me; as I went in and out of the various shops he would calmly sit and wait outside without a word being spoken, until I got to the pub, and he would walk in without hesitation as if it was his second home. The pubs in north Queensland were a joy to behold, hardly anyone wore shoes; they had gone barefoot for so long most of them had what I called Queensland feet: soles as tough as leather that didn't need shoes. Schultz would happily stand there while his owner picked the ticks off him and stamped them on the floor while chatting with his mates as if it was perfectly normal, which of course, for them it was.

Anyway, Schultz was the pack leader and there was never any trouble, at least until Ben came on the scene. Ben was a dog in his prime and had no intention of submitting to Schultz; as soon as we walked into the pub the two dogs started sizing each other up and emitting growls. If there's one thing a Queenslander cannot put up with it is something interrupting his drinking, so it was not long before someone suggested we just chuck the buggers out onto the street and let them sort it out themselves. Nobody objected to this so out we all trotted, the two dogs circled each other a few times before Schultz bit Ben's ear and appeared to flick him onto the ground where he promptly stood over him with his curled lip an inch above poor Ben's throat. Ben instantly relaxed his whole body in submission and ten seconds later we were all back inside. The two dogs got on marvellously after that and I can still remember Mick and I jumping into the wagon on our way to work while Schulz and Ben would chase after us until we'd picked up speed, then off they'd go for the day before returning to meet us in the late afternoon.

On my last night we said our goodbyes over numerous beers and, with a drink-induced melancholy, Mick, who used to wear a shark tooth earring in each ear, insisted I have one of them.

Being as inebriated as he was, I saw this as a gesture of friendship and accepted it in the manner in which it was given. The next morning found me with a hangover and a distinct tilt of my head to the left as the shark tooth swung freely in the breeze; in this delicate condition I carefully boarded the Sunlander Express train for Brisbane where there was a 747 waiting to fly me back to Blighty and a new beginning.

'Tis all a chequer board of nights and days, where Destiny, with men for pieces, plays; hither and thither moves, and mates, and slays – then one by one back in the closet lays. Omar Khayyam

11
London calling

In London, my first port of call was the Transatlantic Hostel in Pimlico, the night receptionist cum general dogsbody was none other than a Kiwi, Morry O'Sullivan, my old drinking partner and fellow barman from the Menzies Hotel in Sydney. Inevitably, the next couple of days were spent indulging our mutual love of beer and bars, and in this endeavour we staggered from the Chelsea Drugstore pub in the Kings Road to The Shakespeare's Head in Carnaby Street, reminiscing about nights out in Sydney. As Mick was a good friend to both of us, it seemed a bright idea for me to give Morry the shark's tooth earring, which entailed a quick pit stop at Kings Cross to get the requisite hole in his earlobe before he could wear the adornment with pride, or at least until he sobered up. I never saw Morry again, he left shortly afterwards to return to Auckland.

I was still no wiser than when I left as to which direction my life should take so I offered to run my parents newsagents business for a while to give them a break. I'd been home about five or six weeks when the phone rang and a familiar voice spouted out, "G'day y'ol' bastard, how ya doin'?" It was Mick, he'd earned enough at the mill to try his luck over here; he was in Amsterdam but was flying to London the following day and wanted to set up a reunion. I should have known the likely outcome but went ahead regardless: the script had already been written. We met, spent all day drinking and continued well into the night, until reaching Piccadilly Circus where I tried to buy a hot dog from a street vendor. He asked for an outrageous amount and I refused to pay; I wasn't a wealthy philanthropic tourist and refused to be treated like one, so I gave him the hot dog back, minus a bite! He took umbrage, waved his knife at me in a threatening manner and following a brief altercation, I was arrested and taken to the local police station; my protestations that the vendor should be arrested for attempted robbery with aggravation fell on deaf ears! Now I had two problems: firstly, I was locked up, and secondly, I was meant to be on the paper train back to Somerset to open the shop and mark up the papers as I had assured my father I would. The arresting constable was asking me all the usual questions but the last thing I wanted was for any of this to get back to my parents so I was evasive with my answers: "Home address?" – "I haven't got one!", "Place of work?" – "I haven't got a job!" It wasn't long before I was taken to the cells and left to stew. The following morning I appeared in court charged with being drunk and disorderly and as my name was read out followed by the words, 'unemployed and of no fixed abode!' I glanced around to see who it was they were referring to before the penny dropped. I was given a ten pound fine or a day in jail; I paid the fine and caught the next train back to Somerset to face the music. My father was rightly disappointed in me but nowhere near as much as I was with myself. He thought I'd met a girl and enjoyed a night of passion. I never had the heart to tell him the truth; it would have disgusted him even more.

After this, I felt that in order to spare my parents further disappointment it would be better to go and I was soon on the move again. I packed a grip and headed for London but could feel myself pressing the self-destruct button even before I boarded the train; I was aware that I was drinking my life away but the alternative of settling into a normal lifestyle in a boring job was not an option I felt I could live with. The days of five star hotels all round the world were a distant memory and I felt lost.

After a couple of days I found myself in Dock Street in the East End of London, trying to get back to sea. The following day

I was flying out to the Persian Gulf to join an Ultra Large Crude Carrier as an Able Seaman; at over 300,000 tons it was one of the largest ships afloat at that time and a real Supertanker.

My last ship, S.S. Lanistes, 311,883t, Shell tanker (Kees Helder).

I was the only English Able Seaman aboard, most of the others were Somali or Cape Verde, and the atmosphere in the crew bar could not be described as congenial. On one occasion I was working with a Cape Verde seaman, painting the bulkhead from the back of the bridge down to the deck, a sheer drop of about sixty feet, and we were gradually lowering ourselves down on a stage as we completed our respective portions. The only thing stopping us from a bone crunching freefall were a few turns of rope around each end of the stage. I was painting the corner which had two external downpipes and had to keep alternating from roller to brush to reach the fiddly bits, while the other sailor was rolling paint onto a flat surface and had to wait each time for me to finish. He made his annoyance obvious and took to undoing the turns on his end of the stage in a petulant display that he was about to start lowering his end. The red mist descended and I shouted at him that if he was in such a bloody hurry I was happy to help and started vigorously throwing the turns off my end in a suicidal manner. The stage tilted alarmingly and he panicked, realising that he may have misjudged the situation, pleading for calm and apologising profusely. He never tried that stunt again.

Realising I had made an error of judgment in going back to sea I sought amends by jumping ship when we arrived in Rotterdam, and caught the train into Amsterdam. Tired and with nowhere to stay I wandered into a little backstreet bar advertising rooms, ordered a beer, sat in the empty bar, and asked the barman if he had any vacancies. At first he said no, but relented after I'd had a couple more drinks and said that there was a room if I did not mind sharing. In truth, I was so tired I didn't care if the other occupants indulged in a full blown, drug-fuelled orgy, so I happily accepted. I turned in shortly afterward but it was such a seedy place I kept my clothes on and slept on top of the bed. In the early hours I woke and heard music coming from the bar downstairs, glanced over to the sink and saw a man injecting himself, but was so drowsy I fell straight back to sleep. I got up about six, saw the junkie snoring contentedly on his bunk, and washed myself before leaving. Downstairs, I entered the bar to find about a dozen people, all stark naked and entwined with each other, fast asleep. I picked my way through the bodies and out into the street, disappointed that I'd missed the action because I went to bed early!

Back in London I needed a job fast and got one that day as a cocktail barman at the Central City Hotel in the Angel. At the interview I apologised for my appearance which, although perfectly suited for the deck of a ship, lacked the style and elegance expected of a cocktail barman. I explained that I had just paid off ship and my luggage had gone astray, which was not a million miles from the truth, and more appropriately attired, I started work the next day.

I initially started in the Tavern bar, more a pub than a hotel bar; the work wasn't overly demanding and the clientele were mainly locals so I could share a laugh and a joke with most of the customers. Nevertheless, it wasn't long before I had a run-in with the management when we cashed up the till and found it was about two pounds short, most unusual, but we had been very busy and a mistake must have been made. The duty manager informed me that the barmaid and I would have to pay the missing two pounds from our wages. Despite my protests that it never went the other way if the till was over, he was adamant we would have to pay, so we did, but the fool never realised how much that would cost him in the long run. To cheat a till and pocket the money was easy, this was before the days of computers and CCTV cameras, and any sense of loyalty I had to the hotel had just evaporated. From that day on, he never once stopped to consider why the till was always over. It was no surprise that the hotel was in the hands of the receivers with that standard of management.

On the occasional evening two fellows would come in for a quiet drink or two: an elderly gent and a younger Scot in his thirties called John. I joked around with them but no more than anybody else. One morning I stopped in the bar for a coffee on my way out; it was convenient because I was 'living in' and my room was in the same block. John came in for a beer and after we had chatted for a time he asked if I fancied going up west with him; as I was not on duty until later that evening it seemed a good idea. We jumped on the bus and half way there he said, "I'd better tell you, I'm over the fence!" Well, I wasn't up to date with all the latest jargon but I guessed that meant he was gay; I told him I wasn't and that was the end of it. He had long ginger hair and wore yellow-tinted glasses which you might imagine would make him look ridiculous even in the 70's, but in actual fact he was always smartly dressed and carried it off with panache. His strong Glaswegian accent ensured nobody within earshot ever took the piss. He was an interesting guy who had been a relief manager for one of the major brewers and knew the West End like the back of his hand. He introduced me to illegal drinking dens of an afternoon, when the pubs were all meant to be shut, and a multitude of Soho characters, including a Maltese strip club owner and his minder, Oma. Soho now is an out and out gay centre but in the seventies it was not so openly flaunted, although you didn't have to sit for long in pubs like the Admiral Duncan or the Golden Lion to realise something was afoot! I'll always remember standing with John at the bar of the Golden Lion when a couple of outrageous guys minced up and ordered two gin and tonics, he turned to me and said, "Would you just look at the state of those queens!" which I found a bit ironic.

John and I used to meet up for a pint pretty regularly and it turns out that the older gent, who was putting John up at his flat, thought that there was something going on between us, which there patently wasn't. One night I'd left John quite early and when I arrived back at the hotel in the early hours of the morning I found a message for me to ring a local police station; given the time, I didn't bother. It transpired that John had returned home, had a huge row with his flat mate, and stabbed him! He was subsequently released on bail and started working at the Swiss Tavern, where the landlord helped him to sort out a brief.

In the meantime I had been promoted to the cocktail bar, an altogether more exclusive clientele, well......at those prices it had to be. The hotel had an arrangement with a Scandinavian travel agency so the majority of the guests were young Scandinavians. I lived in the staff block and one night the duty security guard thought he saw me taking a guest into my room, strictly forbidden, and proceeded to bang on my door requesting entry. I find such people pathetic and told him to go away and get a life, in no uncertain terms. While I was working my shift the following day the Food and Beverage Manager's secretary came up and gave me a written warning about my behaviour: I took it straight to his office, screwed it up in front of him, threw it on the floor and told him I'd be finishing up at the end of the week. It had been a fun few weeks but I wasn't prepared to put up with that level of bullshit.

I went down to Plymouth for a breath of sea air and to recharge my batteries; a few weeks at the Continental Hotel serving drinks to the guests, a stint in a wine bar and a month doing van deliveries in Cornwall, then back to the bright lights, where I left my bag with John at the Swiss Tavern while I sought gainful employment. By now my technique was so polished I had a job within hours: barman again, this time at the Blue Posts pub in Berner Street; not my cup of tea but needs must. Towards the end of the first week I was offered what was billed as a much more attractive proposition at a hotel in the Cromwell Road catering for Aussie and Kiwi backpackers, so I gave a week's notice and started there. I was offered the position by the manager and hadn't met the owners who, I was soon to discover, were a pair of fellows who held themselves in such high regard that the minions were expected to pander to their every whim; the omens were not looking good for me. When I was paid on Friday I found they had made a deduction for living in, which I had not been told about, and which meant I was no better off than my previous job. When I mentioned this it was dismissed abruptly as insignificant, which it may have been for them, but not for me. Their attitude was very much 'take it or leave it', which varied slightly from my own which was more akin to 'take it and leave!' That night as I worked the late shift, I helped myself to a few drinks on the house, then a few more, then discreetly took from the till what I felt I had been cheated out of and told the other barman I was going to the toilet. I picked up my already packed grip from my room, wandered out of the front door and into a balmy summer night and then wondered what the hell I was going to do next. Things were not looking good and there was no prospect of any immediate improvement. My first concern was where to sleep for the night, or what was left of it, and the answer came to me as I strolled slowly up the Cromwell Road.

Opposite the Penta Hotel was a coach park. It was very late, and quiet, and in my inebriated condition it made perfect sense to sleep under a coach using my grip as a pillow. I was asleep in no time at all and enjoyed a few hours before being rudely awakened by the revving of engines; I opened my eyes and, when I saw wheels, I thought I'd been run over, until the memories of the previous night gradually started to unfold. As I struggled out from beneath the coach and brushed myself down I got more than a few bemused looks from the drivers preparing for the day.

While I'd been working at the Blue Posts pub, I would take my breaks in a bar around the corner in Soho called Crackers, and there I had made the acquaintance of an amiable Australian couple: Doug, another blonde, laid back Queenslander who was the bar manager, and Vicki, a Sydney lass with a dry wit, a ready smile and an affectionate nature. I knew the pub had just started doing punk rock in a big way and thought there was a possibility they might need staff. I went straight there and, as luck would have it, one of the full time barmaids had just taken long term sick leave. I started the same day.

The downstairs club was renamed 'Vortex' for Monday and Tuesday nights; it was July 1977, Punk rock was just starting to explode onto the scene and Vortex was the Mecca for Punk bands. It would be heaving with fans dressed to shock, and more piercings than I'd ever seen before; half a dozen studs in the average ear with a chain joining them to a safety pin in the nose or cheek. Faces with more make up than a Christmas panto, and hair, well, spikes were the order of the day, three inch plus spikes on top and shaved at the sides. Then there were the clothes: the more rips, tears, zips and safety pins the better! The place became a ruin, you had to hold your jeans up when you went to the toilet because there was piss all over the place, and spit, I nearly forgot, they loved to spit! It was a tough battle for the cleaners, a quintessential cockney Alf and his son, "I'm bloody cream crackered, never seen anything like it." Twelve years later, I met Alf again purely by chance in a north Cornwall pub; he had sold his cleaning business and bought a hotel in Port Isaac, "Like the blitz, son, lucky to get out alive."

With customers like these, whose creed was 'destroy', 'chaos' and 'anarchy', and bands beseeching their fans to cause mayhem, a certain type of bouncer was required. Nowadays bouncers are all licenced and scrutinised by CCTV, but in those days the majority were only too keen to get stuck in and sort things out

138

with their fists. I always remember one of them; he used to have chilli seeds in his breast pocket and if someone needed escorting off the premises he would lick his fingers, stick them into the chilli seeds, then saunter over to the trouble maker in a non-threatening manner before jabbing his fingers in their eyes. The end result was the person in question staggering blindly up Wardour Street rubbing their eyes furiously and cursing revenge, they were probably half way to Hackney before they could even open their eyes.

Nobody was immune to the violence, it seemed to me that the vast majority of these Punks felt they could spit, swear and act like hooligans without any repercussions, but there is a price to be paid if you want to destroy everything. You do not have to look far on the internet to find a description of what happened when one of the girls in the 'The Slits' decided to relieve herself on the Vortex stage. When a bouncer pointed out this was not acceptable, she bit him, which was the last thing she did for a while because he promptly knocked her out!

Vortex itself was run by an ex-soldier called John Miller who was to become famous a few years later for kidnapping Ronnie Biggs from Brasil: he was one of life's chancers and not afraid to take risks, I think 'colourful' is the expression that springs to mind.

There was one small problem: I had to work a week in hand and my funds were running very low. I managed to get some food while working; the menu was limited to shepherd's pie or frozen pizza but I was not in a position to be choosey, and there was beer a plenty, but it was the sleeping arrangements, or rather the lack of them, that was the hitch. You would think that by this stage of my life I would have no pride left, but I could not bring myself to admit to Doug that I was so broke I needed a sub on my wages. Every night as the staff got into taxis to take them home, I would walk down Piccadilly and sleep on a bench in Hyde Park; if I finished before midnight I sometimes went to Pimlico and paid for a mattress on the floor of a hostel. One balmy evening, I stretched out on a bench in the park and was just dropping off when I heard footsteps on the path walking purposefully towards me. I lay there as the footsteps got closer, and louder, before deciding that discretion was the better part of valour; I jumped up quickly and started hot footing it in the opposite direction. After a short sprint, I looked over my shoulder to see if the assailant was gaining on me only to see a figure running equally fast in the opposite direction! I felt I would look for somewhere else to get some sleep and was walking back down Piccadilly when a Rolls Royce pulled over and beckoned me to jump in. I carried on walking but he drove slowly alongside and continued to gesture for me to get in. I put my head down to the open window and advised the driver in the strongest possible terms that if he valued his health it might be a good idea to engage second gear and get moving. London, like all cities, has a dark underbelly which can be very unnerving for the best of us; youngsters who run away to the bright lights must be easy prey for perverts. Still unsure where I was going, I sat down in a doorway and leant back on the door which promptly opened. I looked in on a plush carpeted stairway; it was clearly not someone's home so I crept upstairs to find a large office that seemed tastefully decorated as far as I could see in the dark. I'd no experience of burglary but I thought it best not to put the light on and I hadn't come in to steal anything, just get some sleep, so I stretched out on the thick carpet behind a desk and was soon fast asleep with every intention of being up and away before the workers arrived. I had no idea of the time cleaners start work in these places until I was rudely awoken by the sound of a vacuum cleaner. It took me a few seconds to remember where I was before I calmly stood up, said a polite "Good Morning" to Mrs. Mop and disappeared down the stairs without a backward glance.

On the nights I slept rough I used to go to the station to shower and get a change of clothes from the bag I kept in left luggage; I may have been living like a tramp but I managed to keep up some standards. Half way through the second week Vicki found out what I was doing and, as the friend she shared her bed-sit with had gone travelling around Europe, offered me the use of the spare bed. It was an act of kindness which came at a low point in my life and one I have never forgotten. I moved in with Vicki and once I picked up my wages I was on easy street again. The money was good because the hours were long: I'd start at eleven in the morning and finish about midnight; on Mondays and Tuesdays I'd work until two thirty or three in the morning. I had a couple of hours or so free in the afternoons, and weekends off to recover!

The next four months or so were a wild, hectic and hilarious adventure through the punk scene and Soho culture. I'd meet up with the Maltese strip club owner, Julie (it seemed rude to ask what it was short for), and his minder, Oma, a huge black fellow who was always immaculately turned out in a suit. We'd drink in the Swiss Tavern in Old Compton Street just a stone's throw from Crackers, when it was a proper pub not the 'swinging' place it has since become, and sometimes in his strip club. His club was what is known as a 'near beer joint' which meant that it did not have a licence to sell alcohol so people only got 'near beer', although they were charged champagne prices. There were always a few cases of the real stuff under the counter for Julie and his mates and Oma handled any complaints, which effectively meant there never were any. It often reminded me of the time Simon and I got ripped off in Yokohama, only this time I was on the other side of the fence, an altogether better position. Some of the guys they introduced me to were serious villains, great fun for a social drink but best kept at arm's length if you wanted to avoid the inevitable prison sentences that go with their lifestyle. I remember one character quite vividly. Oma introduced me to him in the Swiss and he was a genuine East End tough nut but looked unremarkable if you didn't know him. It almost proved to be a fatal error for an Aussie backpacker in an Earl's Court pub. At that time, Earl's Court was known in London as Little Australia for obvious reasons, and this particular Antipodean decided to perform in front of his mates and nudged the little East Ender from behind, spilling some of his beer. The cockney ignored him thinking it was an accident but when it happened again and he turned round to find the Aussies laughing he felt obliged to treat the lad to some manners. He asked him to step outside for a minute and, as the Australian was considerably larger and felt confident he could handle the situation, he obliged. It was only when the cockney pulled out a shooter and stuck the barrel up his nostril that he realised he may have misjudged the situation. By all accounts he returned to the pub with a face as white as a sheet and in need of clean underwear!

John was still working at the Swiss, he'd recently been given a suspended sentence for his misdeeds, and I recall one busy afternoon sitting having a pint near three businessmen in pinstriped suits who were knocking back G&T's, when one of them clicked his fingers at John for service, to which John politely responded by asking him not to. The businessman felt he was not getting the preferential treatment he deserved and told John, "I'll click my fingers at who I like!", at which point John leant right over the bar, put his finger about one inch from the fellow's nose and said in a broad Glasgow accent, "Well, this is one fuckin' monkey you dinnae click yer fingers at!", which pretty much settled the matter.

It had been a roller coaster ride at Crackers, and certainly a memorable experience to witness the Punk explosion. Vortex lasted a mere nine months but in that time it put on the greatest Punk bills of the seventies, and the production of an album, Live at The Vortex, assured its place as a legendary punk venue. It finally closed its doors early in 1978 and I can say without hesitation that I personally thought the music was atrocious, like a cat being strangled but without the melodic tones. One disturbing memory of Vortex was the night Elvis Presley died: the place was in full swing when his demise was announced over the microphone and the punks greeted the news with celebratory cheering; it was sobering, slightly sad, and quite surreal.

As summer drifted into autumn I felt it best to move on again. Doug, Vicki and I went to Paris together, then split up and arranged to meet again on the French Riviera, but the hitchhiking was lousy and I gave up. So I drifted back to Plymouth, my spiritual home, and secured a job labouring in Her Majesty's dockyard, working on a huge contract for building new submarine pens. There were so many people working there that it was quite chaotic; often we could do nothing as we waited for another contractor to finish their job before we could start our own work. I would walk around with an empty bucket trying to look busy or hide away in the engine rooms of the lift shafts playing cards. There was one fundamental flaw in this employment, the distinct lack of alcoholic refreshment; it was also starting to get bloody cold as winter approached.

It did not take much thought to conclude that my life was in a downward spiral of two-bit jobs with no prospects; I wanted to get out of this self-perpetuating circle but could not afford to be out of a job, and had no useful qualifications. I needed a plan and soon came up with one.

Vortex flyer, 1977 (Photo by Paul Wright).

The moving finger writes; and, having writ, moves on; nor all thy piety nor wit, shall lure it back to cancel half a line, nor all thy tears wash out a word of it.

Omar Khayyam

12
Take Courage!

My search for a career that promised stability and fulfilment continued. The Army appeared to offer a solution: I would join the Royal Engineers for three years, learn how to become a civil engineer, come out and get a good job. In reality it wasn't that easy; I was told by Army recruitment that to become a civil engineer I would need to sign for at least six years and, even then, there was no guarantee that I would be chosen for that particular trade. This was not what I wanted to hear, but the results of a recruitment test suggested I should consider Army Intelligence, an imposing title that hinted at an amusing contradiction in terms. I agreed and was sent to Ashford in Kent for two days of tests, and my suspicions about the efficiency of Army Intelligence were raised immediately upon arrival. I had been instructed to catch a certain train from London and advised I would be met on arrival at Ashford station; I duly caught the train in question but there was nobody waiting at Ashford. When I rang the base they explained that they had presumed I would be catching the later 'fast' train which arrived earlier, and so they had returned to the camp! As I had not even set foot on the base I felt now was probably not the best time to enquire as to why I was not simply instructed to catch the other train, and as for presumption, I thought they would have learned a memorable lesson after presuming the Japanese would attack Singapore from the sea! My first impressions could not have been less encouraging, but I'd come this far and thought I might as well see it through.

I spent a couple of days undergoing language aptitude tests and the like and must confess I envisaged myself really enjoying the work; I was using my brain for the first time in years and was revelling in the challenge. I was advised that I had passed all the relevant tests and all I needed now was a security clearance which I was warned might take some time due to my extensive travels and numerous jobs; in the meantime, I needed an income while I waited.

The answer came, as so often in the past, in the licensed trade; I became bar manager at the Drumbeat Club, H.M.S. Drake, in the honourable employ of the Navy, Army and Air Force Institute, or NAAFI as it was fondly known by the military. It was also rumoured that the letters actually stood for No Ambition And Fuck all Interest, but I tried not to take it personally. I lived on the base, which was warm with plenty of good food and beer on tap: I am easily pleased despite the occasional lapse. The job itself was a breeze, being on a naval base meant that if any of the sailors caused a problem they would rapidly find themselves in trouble with the naval police, so there were no problems. After a few weeks, I rang the Army to see how things were developing but there was little sign of any progress, and when after four months I received a letter pointing out that, as I was born in Brasil, they would have to make even more enquiries, my initial suspicions concerning Army Intelligence were confirmed: I must have filled in twenty forms over the previous six months with my place of birth clearly marked, and they had only just noticed!?! The eventual end to my doomed flirtation with Army Intelligence came a full nine months later when I finally received my security clearance, but after such a long period it almost felt like an insult and I didn't even briefly consider replying.

Back in Plymouth and reunited with my long suffering fiancée, I had tired of moving and yearned for stability, and my parents wanted me to run the newsagency while they took a back seat. The outcome seemed inevitable: I got married and took over my parents business. As an indication of confidence in my intention to settle I even bought my first dog but, unbeknown to me at the time, such gestures would ultimately prove to be futile.

I tried hard to make a success of the business but there were just too many obstacles. It is difficult enough at the best of times working with family, but it was a small shop and my father, naturally, wanted things done his way. I fully appreciated that, but in the end I became just a glorified shop assistant, in a little village, in the middle of nowhere. I used humour with the customers in an effort to keep my sanity but it was difficult to empathise with their narrow perspective and mundane lives. If one of the weekly women's magazines was late arriving, or if somebody received the Daily Mail in error rather than their usual Daily Telegraph, they would come straight to the shop to complain and demand an explanation. On occasions, it seemed that it was all they lived for, and looking back, perhaps for some it was.

This was not how I intended to spend the rest of my life, but now I was moving on with a wife and a dog. The dog was a German shepherd that was frightened of his own shadow, but I loved him none the less. We moved to Bristol, a larger and more vibrant city that offered greater hope of employment, and I started work for a small security company that specialised in dogs, but in all honesty it was more like Billy Smart's circus: none of the dogs were trained and some were just undeniably dangerous. I would drive more than two hundred miles a night, checking office blocks and warehouses for twelve hours every night, and then try and sleep in a rundown bed and breakfast that only allowed me to keep the dog there because they had the builders in. I had very little sleep and was chronically exhausted.

Apart from long and anti-social hours, security work is low paid and generally pretty boring. Nowadays, security guards have to be vetted and have a licence from the Security Industry Authority, but in 1980 you were OK as long as you could walk and count to ten, hence the reason I was accepted along with all the other cowboys in the company. The fact that we were entrusted with keys to everywhere shows that an enormous amount of faith was placed in us; it is not for me to suggest that it may have been misplaced.

There is something about being alone in a warehouse in the middle of the night that keeps you on your toes. One particular site we had to visit about three times a night was a tea warehouse on a lonely stretch of road leading from Avonmouth docks; we had to unlock the gate to get in and close it behind us so no opportunistic thieves who stopped by would find it open. In effect, we were locked in and certainly not in a position to make a hasty exit in the event of disturbing someone, and on a wet, dark and windy night in the middle of nowhere, these thoughts are apt to cross your mind! It was on such a night at the tea warehouse, my first stop of the evening, when I found one of the huge, hanger doors partly open. There may well have been a straightforward explanation: perhaps one of the workers simply forgot to close it when leaving, but it was also possible that a gang of thieves intent on mischief had entered. We were not allowed to take our dogs out at this site to avoid the risk of contamination, which made perfect sense but left me the options of either ignoring the rules or just pulling the door closed and leaving quietly, because one thing was certain: I was not going inside without the dog! In the end I took the dog and just steered clear of tea bags for a couple of months.

Things started to look up, I moved out of the bed and breakfast and into a small flat over a barber shop, so at least I could get a few hours kip during the day. Every evening I had to pick up another guard and his dog and take them to their place of work, a huge bus depot, as public transport was not an option. They made a decidedly amusing couple, Lanky was about six feet four inches and slim, and the company had given him a German shepherd bitch they had rescued from death row. The dog was small for the breed and exceptionally vicious, and looked like a rabid fox on the end of the lead; her excessive barking caused froth to form around her mouth which added to the image. Transporting the pair was not as straightforward as you might imagine, my van did not have cages in the back, there was just the one compartment and my dog was in that. This left the driver's cabin for the three of us: me, Lanky and the rabid fox. If Lanky had possessed an iota of common sense he would have placed himself next to me and kept the dog against the door, but, alas, he had total faith that all was OK and let her jump straight in. It concentrates the mind marvellously to have a set of snarling teeth inches from your face; I was never more relieved than when they both got out.

None of the dogs were trained in any way, shape or form, a company philosophy based on the belief that their mere presence would have the desired effect, which it did, but it also meant that there was always the risk of innocent people being bitten. This was before 'No Win, No Fee' lawyers made a triumphal entrance onto the world stage and changed everything; they could have made a small fortune from all the nips inflicted in the name of security.

One of the sites we had to patrol was the all night bus station which almost wholly involved keeping the tramps and drunks out. It sounded simple enough but some of these tramps could get their sleeping bags out and fall soundly asleep in the time it took to walk from one side of the platform to the other; trying to wake them from a deep slumber, often induced by a bottle of chilled meths, sometimes proved tricky. Situations like this have always intrigued me; the general public are not prepared to endure drunks and tramps imposing their unwanted and colourful language on them while they wait for their bus or train, yet they are not willing to do anything about it themselves other than mutter under their breath to each other. They expect somebody else to sort it out, and I know from experience that when someone is utterly intoxicated it is impossible to converse sensibly with them, so that leaves two choices: the police, or a bit of manhandling which can, and often does, escalate. The villain of the piece invariably does not want to leave, and under the influence of alcohol or drugs believes they are more than capable of standing their ground, despite their lack of control over bodily functions. The police do not want the inconvenience of these misdemeanours and even if they do finally put in an appearance, they seldom do anything as it would not be worth the paperwork. They know that locking the person up leads to release next morning and a return performance the following night. If you physically drag someone away the general public mutter "Did you really have to be so hard on them?" failing to recognise that it is concern for their well-being that initiated the whole process in the first place!

There was never going to be any future for me in this job so I applied for every sales vacancy I saw advertised in the local newspaper; I figured that as I seemed to have some measure of ability to talk people round to my way of thinking then I should at least try and get some benefit from it. Eventually, my persistence paid off and I secured a job selling glass washer machines to pubs and clubs. Soon I was driving all over the South West in a company car as one of their top performers producing good sales from the word go; the only possible downside was that I had no relevant technical knowledge, putting a plug on the machines was the limit of my prowess, but this posed no real problems as the average landlord was no better informed than me. I sold one of our largest models to a busy club in Bristol and when I rang my manager with the good news, he asked me if I had informed the club that they would be putting two big three kilowatt heaters onto their ring main system; even if I had known it certainly wouldn't have been top of my sales pitch, I have always tried to keep things as simple as possible, as much for my benefit as anyone else's.

On one occasion, I sold all my machines and drove to head office in Farnborough to stock up. There I met with one of the other salesmen who was also ex-Merchant Navy, and we went for what was intended to be a quick pint. Unfortunately, I still had the monkey on my back and the quick pint ended up as ten. I attempted to drive home and made it as far as Bath before I fell asleep and spectacularly rolled the car, which was only about six weeks old, from the fast lane right across the motorway and up the embankment. I scrambled out and grabbed my ever present tube of extra strong mints in an effort to mask my breath before speaking. Quite a few cars had pulled over by the time the police arrived and I remember thinking that I needed to get down to the police car before they got out and smelled my breath. The general consensus seemed to be that I had had a blowout and I felt it wise to go along with that despite knowing it to be totally untrue. I leant against the police car and assured them I was OK and when asked, I told them that I had not had a drink and had just come from the office. It was about four in the afternoon and they did not suspect anything. They arranged for a tow and instructed me to sit on the bonnet while waiting for the vehicle to arrive. After they departed the adrenaline that had been pumping frantically round my system and helping to maintain the appearance of sobriety seemed to evaporate and I slumped back into a drunken stupor. I told the driver of the recovery vehicle that it was shock kicking in and he seemed to accept that explanation. The traffic policeman who had been on the scene rang next morning to see how I was, he said that I was lucky to be alive and he bet I had a headache. I had a headache alright, an almighty hangover. But here's the nub of the story, in the company's monthly newsletter it said, and I quote, "Top salesman again this month was John Moxley, who was seventeen percent over target and did a victory roll on the M4 to celebrate!"

Herein lay the dilemma: I had a drink problem of which there was no doubt, but because I tended to be successful in my work, people were prepared to indulge my excesses as long as the business kept rolling in. Well, the business kept rolling in and so I kept drinking, and, fortunately or unfortunately depending on your perspective, a bright future lay ahead of me.

By this time my wife was pregnant and as our flat only had one bedroom, we decided to buy a small house. The Building Society was concerned that my commission-based income could not be guaranteed and as a result they were prepared to lend us barely enough to buy a glorified hen house in a rundown area of town. It turned out to be a disaster. It was a small terraced property with the bathroom downstairs and after a heavy rainfall we would have an inch of water sloshing around the floor. Within a few weeks the damp patches started to show through the walls, timed to coincide with the birth of my daughter. So, I now had a wreck of a house, a mortgage that I would have to pay off on my own as my wife was no longer able to work, and another mouth to feed. I was driving hundreds of miles a week; from Bristol I covered an area that included the Isle of Wight and Penzance and it was not unusual for me to be on the road at 5am for an appointment at a pub in Cornwall, get back in the late afternoon having not sold a thing, and therefore, not made a penny. The next day, as likely as not, I'd be on my way down to Bournemouth, or across to Barnstaple, always optimistic that I'd make a sale or two.

As it was I managed to keep the sales up and life wasn't bad but, as usual, reality was about to bite me on the backside, hard. It was the winter of 1981 and the snow came down with a vengeance, transforming even our scruffy little street into something verging on beautiful. As I went up to bed that night I looked in on our daughter and got the shock of my life, water was literally running down the walls. I climbed up into the attic and found that snow had somehow blown into the roof space and was now melting; then the weight of it brought down the ceiling in the airing cupboard! When the snow finally disappeared I had the roof fixed but my torment was only just beginning. The local council owned the property next door and when we moved in it had been occupied by an elderly couple. They had since been rehoused and the new occupants were a young idiot with the IQ of a cucumber, his girlfriend, who made him look intelligent, and their baby. They were insufferable. I have never, before or since, seen such depraved behaviour. The place became home to every lout between the ages of nine and fifteen in the locale as they partied non-stop on their benefits money. Inevitably, they couldn't pay their bills and, I was led to believe at the time, their gas supply was cut off as a result. The idiot's solution to this minor setback was as predictable as it was foolhardy: he promptly tore up the floorboards and lit a bonfire in the house!

It must have been about one or two in the morning when I was woken up by a voice screaming for help. I jumped out of bed and could see smoke coming from next door. I got my wife to take care of our daughter and ring the fire brigade while I quickly packed any belongings I considered essential, grabbed the dog and threw everything into the car. When my wife asked me what I was going to do about the fellow screaming, I was tempted to reply, "I'll throw him a can of petrol" which was cheaper in those days, but instead, I pointed out that if I went round there it could present a bigger health hazard as he risked having the living daylights beaten out of him for threatening everything in life I held dear. I figured that if he had the balls to jump, the worst that would happen was he'd break his legs and I, for one, would not lose a moment's sleep. I had written to the council on several occasions about his actions but they cared not a jot that he had brought misery to all the neighbours and one young nurse had been close to a breakdown. It was most reassuring to find there was some truth in the old adage, "What goes around comes around!"

On a more positive note, although the house next door had been gutted the heat from the fire had dried all the damp patches on my adjoining walls. This was closely followed by more good news when I was offered a position as a Salesman with Courage Brewery; after two years selling glass washer machines I was moving up to the real thing: beer! A good salary, a company car and expenses; things were finally starting to come together for me. I was totally confident in my ability to succeed; with a proven track record in both selling to pubs and working in them, I could not wait to make my mark.

Courage had a history going back to 1787 and its Bristol offices were like stepping back in time: the large, wood panelled rooms and corridors exemplified traditions long since lost and inspired you to uphold the standards established over generations. The building has since been gutted and is now an Asda store, where the smell of freshly baked bread has rapidly replaced the dusty aroma of history.

Courage brewery, Bristol (John Law).

From day one the job was like a holiday. I moved up to a lovely new house in Gloucester and soon became well known in just about every Free House and Club in the area. A drink or two at the Restoration Inn in Cheltenham, another couple at the High Roost overlooking the famous racecourse, another here and another there, and all on expenses. This was the daily routine, only the pubs changed, the business kept rolling in and my boss was happy. It did not take me long to establish which landlords enjoyed a drink and I used to finish my calls in these honey pots. The worst of these, or perhaps best, was the Famous Pint Pot in Gloucester, which should have been renamed the Infamous Pint Pot, and it became my second home. The landlord, Barry, another Londoner with marital problems, became a good friend and after the antics we used to get up to in his pub I often wonder how either of us survived. We'd drink all day and well into the evenings, competing in every conceivable pub game and trials of strength with his crowd of locals, invariably ending in various stages of undress while singing rugby songs. Then I would stagger out to the car and drive home; it was often said that it was a good job I was driving because I was in no fit state to walk. This was my average Monday, the start of the week; God alone knows how I used to make it through to Friday.

This was the culture of the brewery trade at that time. I remember one annual conference when we were all booked into the beautiful Thurlestone Hotel in South Devon for a few days. The hotel rests in a small rural village that is set back from the cliffs overlooking the sandy beaches of Thurlestone Bay, the River Avon estuary and Burgh Island. At four in the afternoon we met up in the bar and the company chairman decided we would have a boat race; this is where you line up in teams, one behind the other, each with a pint of Kronenbourg. At the command 'go' the first one drinks his pint as fast as he can and then stands the upturned glass on his head before the next does the same, and so on until you have all finished. After the first race the chairman said that somebody had cheated so we had a rerun, then another. By ten past four we had already had three pints and were expected to go on to the early hours!

The continuing rise in my sales figures mirrored my fall from grace: it was as inevitable as my next beer. I was out every night and it was no surprise that my marriage was failing even though I had a beautiful three year old daughter, blonde hair and blue eyes, who I loved dearly. The breakdown was entirely my fault. I found my only solace in the bottom of a glass which further added to my problems and, as ever, there was never a shortage of drinking partners. Although I was living a pretty unorthodox lifestyle I managed to keep myself fit by running my dog. I have not really mentioned him much but he meant everything to me. He had always been a very nervous dog which I used as an excuse for his behaviour, as you do for a child, until he became so erratic that I sought help. A police dog handler and a local dog trainer who I had turned to for advice both said that he was so unreliable he should be destroyed. I could not accept their decision until the day he completely flipped and made a full attack on me, for no reason whatsoever. The vet agreed it was the best course of action but it still brings tears to my eyes thirty years later. I have since been led to believe it was something called idiopathic aggression, and there was nothing I could have done, but in truth, it does little to ease my feelings of guilt and failure. At first I could not bring myself to get another dog, but my life felt empty without one and I eventually bought a Rottweiler puppy that I named Guinness.

It seems like a world away now but those two years with Courage went by in a haze. I remember once judging a wet t-shirt competition at a nightclub in Bristol, which is quite ironic if you know what Bristol City means in cockney rhyming slang! Nobody had ever trained me for this role, though it was one I was keen to get to grips with, and there seemed to be no set rules on what exactly you were meant to be marking. Was it the size, the shape, or possibly even the movement? There were three judges and the other two were as ignorant of the finer points as I was, it always looks easy when you watch them on Strictly Come Dancing but it's not the same when you have an audience behind you baying the contestants on. If you have never seen how a wet t-shirt competition works it is all reasonably straightforward: the contestants wear the bottom part of a bikini but on the top they are only allowed a t-shirt, invariably with the sponsor's name written across the chest. They step, one at a time, into a paddling pool, where a lucky lad pours ice cold water from a watering can over the front of their t-shirts in an effort to enhance their assets. Within seconds the audience or, to be more precise, the men in the audience, start shouting that they cannot see much because the sponsor's name is in the way, in this particular instance it was Hoffmeister, and invite the ladies to raise their shirts. The ladies tend to oblige in their eagerness to win the substantial prize on offer, which only encourages further cries of, "Higher, higher!" As the competition progresses the shirts get progressively higher in the hopes of influencing the judges: as if! There tended to be two types of women who entered these shenanigans: very attractive girls with aspirations of getting their first step on the ladder to becoming a footballer's wife, and drunks who have entered on the night for a laugh. Well, on this particular night it was going swimmingly and the marks were all pretty close when a buxom brunette came on to the stage, apparently fuelled by more than the odd Babycham, and completely dispensed with the pretence of lifting and lowering the t-shirt and just whipped it straight off. What followed next was an example of bodily control I have never witnessed since, her breasts appeared to possess a will of their own, first one way, then the other, up, down and round and round, how she managed to keep her balance was a marvel and the crowd were roaring their approval. I looked to the senior judge for advice but he was transfixed: as a finale it was hard to beat!

After a couple of years at an unrelenting pace I could no longer carry on as if everything was OK. Although I really enjoyed the job, the management and other reps, I felt I had no option other than to reluctantly tender my resignation. When I went to say farewell to Barry at the Pint Pot, he asked me what I intended to do. I needed a job that offered accommodation to keep me in a position to carry on paying the mortgage so I told him I was going back into the pub trade. As it happened, he had spotted a rundown 'trouble' pub that he felt had a lot of potential and he was looking for somebody to run it, which is how Guinness and I found ourselves billeted over The Pelican Inn in Stroud.

'How sweet is mortal sovereignty!' think some. Others 'How blessed the Paradise to come!' Ah, take the cash in hand and waive the rest, Oh, the brave music of a distant drum!
Omar Khayyam

13
The Pelican brief

My father had felt unwell for some months and when exploratory tests confirmed he had bowel cancer, he had to go to London for a colostomy. My relationship with my father had always been difficult but it didn't stop me loving him; I admired him and was acutely aware that I had not made his life any easier. The pub I had just taken over was closed for refurbishment so I took the opportunity to travel up and see him a couple of days after the operation. It was difficult for me to see him looking so vulnerable and I felt overwhelming guilt that I had been the cause of so much worry for him over the years. The doctors were pleased with the outcome of the procedure but only time would tell how successful it had been; I never took him for granted again.

With my ongoing marriage break-up, taking over a pub was akin to letting a pyromaniac loose in a fireworks factory with a box of matches. Experiencing a crisis of identity coupled with a tendency to drown your sorrows would be a disastrous combination for most jobs but it proved remarkably successful in this environment and trade soon took off. We became one of the 'in' places in town and had a strong following among the locals, who came for the music and late night drinks. Stroud was not an easy place to love, a small market town on the edge of the Cotswold Hills, too big to be a village but without the attractions of a larger town, it felt quite insular, though the locals seemed happy enough which counted in its favour.

I encouraged a local DJ to record music tapes for us and

every now and again he would insert a comical sketch between songs, the locals would know when they were coming and it would all go quiet as the joke played out followed by a burst of laughter as the music kicked in again. He even put 'Nellie the Elephant' on one of the tapes and it was comical to see all the youngsters belting out the words before getting back to their conversations. I had a special tape to put on ten minutes before closing time which included 'Farewell' by Jimmy Ruffin and 'Go Now' by the Moody Blues. This was a trick I had picked up at the Elephant and Castle pub in Sydney, where they always sang 'Show Me the Way to go Home' at the end to let the customers know it was time to leave. It didn't have quite the same effect at The Pelican, and although I made all the right noises and packed off the bulk of the customers, there was always a hard core of locals who stayed on until the early hours.

Of course, while getting a local DJ to make up the tapes was a clever move, it was not the cherry on the cake. As I mentioned previously, the pub was extremely rundown, had virtually no trade and a shocking reputation to boot. The first thing we did when we took over was to close it, give it a lick of paint and a new set of furniture, throw out the juke box and dartboard and install a sound system. A small number of young bikers had made it their local so on opening night I arranged for a few rugby players to be in attendance while I explained to the lads, before they could get through the doors, that no leather jackets were allowed in, and suggested they find a new clubhouse, which they did with hardly a murmur. This left us with a cracking fun pub with absolutely no trouble but, unfortunately, we didn't have any customers either. My ways around this problem were twofold. Firstly, hire a couple of attractive, chatty barmaids; always a good starting point. But the masterstroke was getting the DJ to make up the tapes and advising him that I would have to pay him in beer. DJ's always have a following with local girls and, as he had to drink in my pub, the girls naturally followed, and where the girls go you can rest assured the boys will never be far behind. The tactics worked and the pub went from strength to strength.

One of the funniest incidents came after a few weeks. The pub itself had no garden as such but a large flat roof which Guinness used as her backyard. I used to leave the window open so she could go in or out as she pleased and she would lie on the sofa looking out onto her domain. One day there was a delivery of heating oil and the driver, unaware there had been a change of ownership, leant his ladder against the roof and climbed up onto the top of the oil tank which was the same height and flush with the roof. Guinness must have been asleep and did not hear him, but when he unscrewed the cap and went to insert the hose, the iron coupling banged against the side of the tank. Guinness was out like a shot, with lips curled, and flew straight at the driver, who, despite being in his mid fifties, took one look at her and then jumped clean off the roof. The first I knew of it was when this ashen faced man limped into the pub and asked, "Who owns that fucking wolf on the roof?" The whole pub burst out laughing.

Shortly after I took over The Pelican, my ex-wife and daughter moved back to Plymouth to be close to her family. Once a fortnight I would drive the hundred and thirty plus miles and take my daughter out for the day, and, as any absent father will know only too well, it can be very difficult entertaining a young child under such strained circumstances; there are only so many play areas and McDonalds you can visit. Then came the moment I used to dread, when I had to leave her again; she would be in tears asking why I had to go and why couldn't she have a proper daddy? I used to drive back up the M5 with tears running down my face and, after arriving back at the pub, I would attempt to drown out the guilt with beer; it never worked and I had to learn to live with it. Despite the fact that she has since grown into a beautiful young lady, a gifted teacher and wonderful mother, I still struggle to come to terms with the fact that I walked out on her.

An indication of the depths to which I had sunk was the game of Jacks. Not the game of school playgrounds but a drinking game played by people who, for whatever reason, want to escape the reality of their existence. It involves dealing from a pack of cards and whoever is dealt the first Jack has to nominate a drink, usually an obnoxious mixture of two spirits or liqueurs, the person dealt the second Jack has to pay for it, the third Jack has a sip of the drink and the fourth has to swig the rest down in one go. It was well after closing time one night when a few of us decided to stitch up Mike: a large serving of green washing-up liquid was poured into a glass and placed just behind the Crème de Menthe bottle. The cards were fixed while he answered a call of nature and, on his return, the drink nominated was Baileys and Crème de Menthe and, unsurprisingly, Mike drew the fourth Jack. It was easy enough to switch the glass and just top up the washing up liquid with Baileys, the person who was supposed to sip it deserved an Oscar for his performance and, as we handed the glass to the victim we were all chanting "Down in one, down in one, down in one!" and, as machismo demanded, Mike duly quaffed the mix in one go. He managed to keep it down for about five seconds before disappearing into the toilet at great speed, the rest of us were too busy laughing to appreciate the condition he was in. After a few minutes, we gingerly ventured out to see what had become of him, only to find Mike lying spread-eagle on the floor next to a pan full of vomit and bubbles. He was last seen wandering home up the lane next to the pub as we all sympathetically sang "I'm forever blowing bubbles" at the tops of our voices. The following day, he walked in looking like an apparition and made his way slowly to the bar before announcing "I must have the shiniest arse in Stroud!" and ordering a pint of lager.

Although the previous landlord had his car overturned in the car park, I was pleasantly surprised that despite the pub's reputation as a 'trouble' pub, nobody ever physically threatened me. Of course there were a few incidents, but never a direct challenge. Shortly before I left I discovered a possible reason for this when I mentioned it to one of the locals. He said that once word got round that I used to box for the navy nobody was too keen to have a go, which, while it provided an ideal image for me, was totally untrue. It was the result of a misunderstanding when I first moved in. I had set up a punch bag in the garage and was having a workout, when a passing local interested in the plans for the pub asked me if I boxed and I said no but I did a bit when I was in the navy: and so the lie was born! Of course, I was ably supported by Guinness behind the bar whenever trouble was brewing; it was common knowledge that she took no prisoners.

The New Year brought hopes and desires that were never going to be achieved while I was faced with constant temptation. I now had a girlfriend who, understandably, was not enamoured with my lifestyle and even offered to pay the rent on a flat for us while I got back on my feet. I needed to get out of the pub before it killed me, so I asked Barry to find a replacement and set off to try my luck again in sales. I drove down to Bristol and rented a small bed-sit in one of the less salubrious suburbs. The basement of the converted house was taken up by somebody who had aspirations to be a drummer in a rock band and practiced whenever he could, and the flat above was home to a couple of students who played music until the early hours. It was only a matter of time before I introduced myself and Guinness, who was not officially resident for obvious reasons, to request a little peace: it was around 3am, the students were halfway through a roaring rendition of Pink Floyd's 'Dark side of the Moon' and in the process of rolling up their umpteenth joint. I banged on their door so loudly they thought it was the drug squad and when they saw the Hound of the Baskervilles salivating at my side they promptly lowered the volume. I had little trouble with them after that. Unfortunately, Keith Moon's relative downstairs proved impossible to shut up.

To most people their first day at work is quite traumatic, but I've had so many that to me it's just like a day out. I'd managed to convince a national kitchen company that I could sell their excellent range of kitchens, and I was sent on a residential course in Coventry for a most interesting week of brainwashing. On the final day I was issued with their full range of kitchen doors, some oak, some cherry and some ash, but all very impressive; so many doors, in fact, that it took all my ingenuity to squeeze them into my mini. Early Monday morning I strolled into the Bristol office and was given my first appointment, eight that evening in Hereford; hardly what I would call local. Anyway, never one to shirk a challenge, that January evening found me crossing the Severn Bridge and wending my way through the back of beyond to Hereford. Well, the wind began to blow and the snow began to fall, and carried on falling in ever larger flakes. It began to settle, covering everything in sight. I began to get concerned, and with visions of being stuck in the middle of nowhere I decided to call it a day and headed home. When I went into the office the following morning the sales manager, a plump little Scotsman who suffered from 'small man syndrome', was fuming; it hadn't been snowing in Bristol, so he had a right old go at me, and even when I explained the situation he was still ranting, red-faced and shaking with fury. The temptation to whack him was overwhelming but as I was trying hard to escape my bad boy image, I did the next best thing. I turned round, walked out to my car and disappeared into the sunset with a full set of doors, which would no doubt come in very handy at a later date.

Over the next couple of years I drifted from job to job; a few months selling frozen food: the area manager did not appreciate my reluctance to submit to his authority; best part of a year selling brewery equipment: the equipment was such poor quality that I spent most of my time picking up returns; selling engraving machines to jewellers: I try not to remember the details but.... never again. At the end of my tether, I managed to secure a position selling storage systems to offices, schools and hospitals, which is some indication of the desperation I was beginning to feel. Surprisingly, it proved to be a winner; it was all cold-calling and my sales just took off: I was the star performer. The only salesman who ever beat me was the one who covered London; apart from that I was always top of the tree, usually by a comfortable margin, and I kept all the company statistics as evidence to remind myself that I did have some positive attributes.

Some months previously I had moved out of the flat and rented a farmer's cottage. When I applied for the cottage I conveniently forgot to mention Guinness. The week before I was due to move in and after the agency had checked all my references, I rang the agent and told them that my grandfather had just died and if I didn't have his dog it would have to be destroyed. I told her it was an old Labrador; well, if Guinness had possessed a tail she would have looked a lot like one, and she said it would be OK for us to move in. When Guinness next came into season I decided to breed a litter off her, and what a palaver that was. I took her to a stud dog, but timing is critical and it was a bit too early so she would not mate. The owner of the stud suggested we come back in two or three days but, in the meantime, I had to ensure the bitch was 'broken in'. On enquiring exactly what this meant it was explained to me that some bitches may have a stricture which needs breaking to allow proper mating. It felt like a silly question at the time but I had to ask, how was I supposed to do this? Basically, two fingers and some Vaseline jelly, said in such a manner as to suggest it was common knowledge. When we arrived home I got straight to work, the bitch was perfectly happy with the situation even if I felt more than a bit uncomfortable: I quickly asked my girlfriend to draw the curtains in case somebody saw what was happening and reported me to the RSPCA. This was my first foray into dog breeding and I was not overly impressed so far.

Anyway, it worked, and nine weeks later the results started popping out onto the kitchen floor, all eleven of them: I thought they would never stop. They were soon running around causing mayhem and I was praying the farmer did not put in an appearance. The garden was large and backed onto a field but the fence had a lot of small holes through which the puppies could easily squeeze; what I needed was some kitchen cabinet doors. The doors were ideal, not only were they one hundred percent effective but they also added a splash of colour to the garden. At eight weeks old I sold all the puppies except one, Murphy: he was a bear of a dog. Murphy grew rapidly and when we went out we just left the back door open so he and Guinness had the run of the house and garden; no unwelcome guests would get in with them around.

Business continued to flourish so we moved to Clevedon, a small town near Weston-Super-Mare, once a popular holiday resort but which had seen better days and was now primarily a commuter town for Bristol. We bought a house with a fully enclosed garden and, again, we just left the door open for the dogs to wander in or out. They were big dogs and always had plenty of exercise before we left so, invariably, they just slept until we got back and, as I had this selling job cracked, I was never back very late. On my first day, I returned home to find a letter from the person whose house backed onto mine complaining that he worked from home and could not concentrate as my dogs were constantly barking. I had not had this problem before, so I went straight round to apologise and said they just needed to settle in. The next day, another letter, so I asked the neighbours on either side if they had been disturbed and both assured me they had not; in fact, one was a night worker and slept during the day and had not heard a thing. Round I went again but in absolutely no mood to apologise this time; the fellow answered the door but if he was expecting another grovelling apology he would be sorely disappointed. I asked him if he was sticking his head over the fence, because they were natural guard dogs and would inevitably bark. He assured me that he wasn't, but when I asked him which one was doing all the barking and he answered "The big one!" he must have realised that he had dropped himself in it. I left him with a few carefully chosen words and never heard from him again.

After another hard day on the road I had just returned from Cardiff and was enjoying a cup of tea when the phone rang. It was a recruitment agency I had registered with the previous year, they had a vacancy for a Brewery Salesman and was I interested?

And much as wine has played the Infidel, and robbed me of
my robe of honour – well, I often wonder what the vintners
buy, one half so precious as the goods they sell.
Omar Khayyam

14
Mixing my drinks

Although I would have jumped at an opportunity to return
to the brewery trade, I was not particularly optimistic about my
chances; my CV was beginning to show serious signs of someone
prepared to jump ship at the first hint of trouble, and that was
the 'doctored' CV, the real one had me cringing! I instructed the
recruitment agency to forward my CV to the company and if
they wanted to see me, I would welcome the opportunity. The
company in question was Ushers Brewery, the South West
trading arm of Watneys, and I sailed through the interview. I was
doing well where I was but my income was overwhelmingly
commission-based so the pressure was always on and frankly, I
loved the brewing trade. So it was not a difficult decision to

Ushers brewery offices, Trowbridge (Mark Wheaver).

accept the job but I felt genuinely sorry at leaving; the entire management had been outstanding and I held them in high regard.

I was advised that the area I would be covering had seen seven representatives in two years and sales volume was down by fifteen hundred barrels year on year; with this in mind I was not sure who was more desperate, the company or me. It was perplexing when on my first night out with the sales trainer in Newbury, we called on three pubs only to find that our products had been thrown out of two of them; I was losing accounts before I had even started. However, I revelled in the challenge and threw myself into it wholeheartedly. I relocated to Swindon, a rapidly expanding town as major businesses moved into the area, and a commuter stronghold for both Bristol and London. Once famous solely for its railway works, these had been relegated to museum status as the town rode the wave of modernisation and high employment. Consequently, there was plenty of business to be had, and I had every intention of getting more than my fair share of it. I managed to stop the rot and it wasn't long before the business started to come on board and the sales figures were moving in the right direction. After a year, I won the top salesman award, a five star holiday in the Canaries for my girlfriend and me, and a trip to Brands Hatch for a day racing cars. I was actually enjoying myself and to be totally honest, did not have to work too hard; it was almost too easy. I was seldom home later than two in the afternoon and it would have been earlier if I hadn't stopped for a pint or two over lunch. I also visited clubs in the evenings but it was only a couple of nights a week and hardly a chore.

My sales technique has always been unorthodox: I am very confident and straightforward in my approach and never use ten words when one will do. Some other salesmen would waffle on and on when I just wanted to cut to the chase and get the contract signed. I understood that this was not the typical way companies liked to train their sales force, they liked to ensure that every 'i' was dotted and every 't' crossed, but I found this robotic approach mind-numbing and could not adapt to it. My best results always came when I was left to get on with the job in my own way, without a self-obsessed management control freak riding on my back. If I needed help I was more than happy to ask and never considered it a sign of weakness, otherwise I liked to get on with the job in hand.

Work was going well and I was enjoying it but my problem of drinking to excess remained. It was no longer a case of getting plastered every day but being unable to stop once I had gone past the tipping point and in the brewing industry there were too many opportunities at events that I was expected to regularly attend. I would have loved to avoid them: I find the small talk and obligatory point scoring of such occasions uninspiring and quite negative. Christmas parties were a particular bugbear and seemingly impossible to dodge: when I tried to find an excuse I was accused of being an unsociable old sod along with the inevitable veiled threat that 'I really should attend, bad form not to!' When I did attend, my efforts to make the trivial prattle half-interesting often ended in a drink-fuelled argument and muttered disapproval of my behaviour.

No doubt this leaves an impression that seems at odds with the environment where I spent much of my time, but the fact is that a laugh and a joke with customers was part of my business. I had to earn money and found that my ability to quickly establish a rapport with others could be used to my advantage. This is not to detract from the many genuine friends I made on my travels, of whom I have a multitude of fond memories and who enriched my life immeasurably. Socialising with industry colleagues, on the other hand, falls into the realms of personal relationships and had we not been thrown together by work, I would not have chosen to socialise with many of them as personal friends. My despondency is aimed solely at the tiresome 'jobsworths', whose lives revolve around television soaps and office gossip; who have a wishbone where they should have a backbone. At least I gave them plenty to tittle tattle about!

I had established myself as a successful salesman and got on well with the senior management so when a vacancy arose in Plymouth where I would be closer to my daughter the company were happy for me to relocate. I was eagerly looking forward to moving back to Plymouth when fate cast its shadow. Guinness had developed a particularly aggressive form of cancer and died the week before I moved down, a loss I felt deeply; we had been through so much together.

The move itself was relatively uneventful. My area of work took in the beautifully rugged north Cornwall coast with its secluded sandy coves and rocky cliffs tumbling vertically into the surging emerald Atlantic; I felt privileged to be so lucky. I thought I'd buy another dog to keep Murphy company and purchased an English bull terrier: Duchess was white with red patches on one eye and an ear and looked as if she'd come straight out of a comic cartoon. Initially, Murphy viewed his new canine companion with icy mistrust but after a couple of attempts at taking a chunk out of the Duchess, his suspicions thawed and they became the best of friends.

It was at this time that my girlfriend began to get broody, but children were certainly not high on my agenda, in fact they were not even on the radar: I was still struggling to manage my relationship with my daughter and could not face the possibility of going through it all again. Nevertheless, within a few weeks I had been persuaded and found myself stuttering over the words, "I do." As an added bonus, she had the same name as my first wife so at least my tattoo was still fit for purpose. She was an unpretentious and attractive blonde and a great stabilising influence on me, but without changing my rebellious nature, and without her I dread to think where I would have ended up. We shared a love of dogs and preferred long walks in the country to socialising, and I was lucky she was prepared to accept me so readily.

The wedding was a small affair with only immediate family present. My father's cancer had returned with a vengeance and spread to his brain; I was so pleased that he could make it. He died within the month and was only 63. There were so many things I should have said to him, and wished I had but never did. I understand this is not uncommon to others and wonder why we find it so hard to express our emotions; I guess everyone has their own particular reasons and I think in my case it is the fear of showing weakness and leaving myself open to rejection. His last few days left an indelible impression on me. As those who have watched someone being eaten away by cancer will appreciate, the body is ravaged until it is just skin, bones and sores, and it was while my father was in this state that he managed to utter a few words which still sadden me, "It takes a long time to die!" I remember thinking to myself that if I let one of my dogs suffer like that the RSPCA would have me in court charged with cruelty. I hope that as my last lap approaches the law will recognise my right to choose not only how I live but also how I die and I won't have to travel to Switzerland should I decide to sign off a week or two early, preferably with the aid of a bottle of vintage rum. At least I won't have to worry about the hangover!

Anyway, as often seems to occur in life, just as the engine starts running smoothly something wraps itself around the prop. It started as a rumour and was soon confirmed that Courage would take over Watneys and sell Ushers as a small independent brewery. I could see no positive outcome for me in this arrangement: Courage already had a strong sales force in the South West and Ushers could not be competitive as a small independent: the writing was on the wall. I contacted Bass brewery on the off chance and was offered a sales job with them covering the jewel in Devon's crown, the South Hams: Salcombe, Dartmouth, Dartmoor, Noss Mayo to name just a few of the stunningly attractive towns and areas set among tantalising rolling farmland, coastline and moorland. I offered my resignation to Tony, the Sales Director at Ushers, with deep regret; I loved my job and the people I worked with, and owed a debt of gratitude to Tony for putting up with all my shenanigans during my time there. He wrote me a touching personal letter thanking me for my contribution to the company and said that if things didn't work out he would always take me back. There was more truth in that than he realised at the time. His nickname among the other reps was 'Hatchet man' because if you crossed him there was every likelihood you'd be out of a job, but I got away with murder and, on one occasion, he was literally my 'get out of jail' card!

Bass postcard (Robert Opie collection@Museum of Brands).

Bass was a far more conservative company than Watneys, more prim and proper and far less fun. They thought the strength of their brands was unbeatable and this led to an air of complacency, though they would never admit it; they were slow to realise that the market was changing and this attitude was no longer acceptable.

A particular pub that was always a pleasure to call on was the Rugglestone Inn, a small granite cottage that had been converted to a pub many years ago near Widecombe-in-the-Moor, Dartmoor. It was off the beaten track, nestled in a valley bottom next to a brook, and was run by a magnificent landlady called Audrey. She had inherited the pub from her father and when you entered it was like stepping back to the turn of the century, even Audrey's hair and clothes were reminiscent of that era. There was no bar as such, just a small serving hatch with room enough for one person, and the barrels of beer stacked behind her in what could only be described as a large pantry. There were two small, separate rooms for drinking, which had presumably been a parlour and lounge in a previous life but now had a handful of tables and chairs. The tables were covered in brown oilcloth, a couple of traditional mirrors adorned the walls along with a large, antique clock whose ticking seemed to hang in the air; and that was it. No music, no fruit machine, no food and, if an unsuspecting tourist wandered in and asked for a coffee, they were none too politely advised by Audrey that it wasn't a café. She didn't sell any spirits and God forbid anybody should even think of asking for a lager, the pub sold one beer and one beer only, Draught Bass, straight from the barrel. Draught Bass in South Devon used to be an institution, nearly all the pubs stocked it, and as the Bass representative in the area I was always being asked by the other landlords why their Bass never seemed to taste the same as Audrey's. I fobbed them off with excuses about it coming straight from the barrel but the reality was totally different. The real reason was because Audrey never sold Draught Bass, she sold Charrington IPA, an altogether different brew from London, but as far as Audrey was concerned she bought it from Bass so it was Bass; the deception went on for years until Bass finally stopped brewing Charrington IPA! As you can imagine, Audrey would never even consider anything as modern as a direct debit, so at the end of every month I used to wend my way across the moor to collect the cheque and soak up the atmosphere with her regulars; I remember her telling me once how the moor farmers held on to their wives, "They keep them pregnant in the summer and take their shoes away in the winter!" Shortly after I left she sold the pub, it now does food, coffee, and almost certainly sells lager!

Rugglestone Inn, Dartmoor (Richard & Vicki).

I cannot deny that I had been most fortunate to cover such an area, for sheer beauty and character it was hard to beat, but as there were no major conurbations the potential for growth was severely limited, and I started to get bored. Then some aspiring genius at head office, probably straight from university with a degree in marketing, decided he wanted information on every single outlet that held a licence within each area. The information he required was far more than necessary for effective marketing and the whole project resembled an exercise in scoring brownie points. The final insult came over a pub I knew very well, the

London Inn at Ivybridge. It had been an old Ushers account and at one Christmas party at the pub I had been warmly applauded for my rendition of 'The Wild Rover' and topped the night off by emptying a pint over the landlord's head, although I must stress that he was the instigator of the beer throwing! Anyway, when I advised the mastermind behind this exercise that the pub had since been knocked down and turned into council offices, he had the audacity to send a request for 'more information required'. I'm not sure exactly what was wanted, maybe the colour of the front door or the number of spaces in the car park; my response was both vigorous and acerbic and I never heard from him again.

One of my accounts, Millbrook Inn, Southpool (Ian & Dianna Dent).

I'd just got in after a strenuous afternoon supping ale on the seafront at Dartmouth, when the phone rang. It was Courage brewery, someone called Ian was looking for a Business Development Manager to be based in the Plymouth area and his superior had told him I was the man for the job; he wanted to meet me. It transpired that Tony, the ex-Sales Director from Ushers, was now head of the Business Development team at Courage, a stroke of luck if ever there was one.

It was like returning to the fold when I went back. There were so many faces from my days at both Courage and Ushers that I felt instantly at home. Despite the fact that I had spent years at both companies I still had to go on a three week residential course in Bristol with all the other new Business Development Managers; Courage had decided to have a major sales push and we had been chosen to drive the business forward. In the sales environment you were judged to be either a 'hunter' or a 'farmer', the titles being self explanatory, one excelling at going out to hunt for new business while the boring farmers provided lots of tender, loving care to the existing client base. Hunters, by their very nature, tend to be outgoing and slightly extrovert, so to put twenty of them in a top hotel for three weeks was a recipe for disaster; the first week was spent sounding each other out, the second seeing how far we could push things, and the third served up the coup de grace as, with pants and trousers around our ankles we danced a 'Father Abraham' in the hotel bar. We left ready and eager to make Courage the market leader in the world of beer, and intended to start the minute our hangovers had lifted.

I went after the business in just about every pub and club in South Devon, and met some of the most interesting characters in the industry in the process. One was from a family of some considerable infamy; he wanted to borrow nearly two million pounds to buy a job lot of local pubs that a brewery was selling off. I met him and his board of directors, I use that term loosely, and it was clearly a financial non-starter but I had a gut feeling that if I pointed this fact out I would be found floating past the Eddystone lighthouse on the evening tide. This was not a man to be messed with. I have met many men who are happy to bully, shout and threaten and the majority are usually just wind and piss; he was not one of them! I just prayed that another brewery made them an offer they couldn't refuse.

Another character I came across at this time (I am not naming names because I still live in the area and would like to keep my kneecaps), was the manager of the busiest nightclub on the infamous Union Street. We were in protracted negotiations over the club's business and I was not giving in to his demands as much as he would have liked, so he asked me if I knew who he was before answering the question himself and informing me that he 'ran' Plymouth. Always a hostage to hazardous humour, I replied that I thought a certain family (see previous paragraph) held that position, to which he replied that they used to, but now it was him. As I was dealing with such royalty I felt it wise to slack off a bit on my earlier refusal and that, in light of this new information, the brewery would be happy to buy the club some new fridges. We ended up getting on famously and I took all the business from my main competitor, Bass. I can still see him now, a Devon version of Arnold Schwarzenegger; our paths were to cross again in the future, just before he was ordered to spend the first of two, eight year stretches as a guest of Her Majesty.

The job was going extremely well and I was enjoying it again, but even I could see that there was a limit to the business to be had in the area and there were plenty of 'farmers' to look after the accounts I had brought on, so my future was far from certain. On making a few discreet enquiries I established that I was expected to weave my magic in North Devon before moving on to Birmingham. South Devon is one thing, but North Devon is a completely different kettle of fish, a breed apart and best kept that way in my opinion; the simple fact that it would take me an hour and a half to drive up there did not ignite my enthusiasm. I gave it ten minutes deliberation before tendering my resignation. The next day Tony phoned: he'd just heard the news and wondered what the problem was. I explained that I had no grievances whatsoever, fully understood the thinking behind their plans, but it was not for me and so I was off. He asked me what I intended doing and as it was summer I flippantly replied that I'd be going to the beach. When he asked what I'd do in the winter, I said I'd worry about that then. He laughed, said I'd never change, and we parted as friends.

Of course, this was all bravado, the reality was somewhat different: by now I had a mortgage, two sons and maintenance to pay, so I needed to do something quickly. It was not long before the phone rang with an offer. The chap on the other end was known to me, an ex-policeman with more neck than Big Ben, as was his financial backer, the Cornish equivalent of Arthur Daley, and he suggested we meet; it could do no harm. Basically, he was fronting what was called a secondary wholesaling business; he had a couple of busy pubs and clubs that, as a result of their high volume of sales, were receiving particularly high levels of discounts. He was prepared to sell some of his beer and lager on to brewery tied pubs at a substantially higher price than he was paying but still considerably lower than the tied pubs would normally have been charged. This resulted in even higher sales and even better discounts but the trouble was that if too much was ordered the brewery would become aware of the operation. He wanted somebody to help source new suppliers and new outlets and, as I knew most of the main players, they thought that I might consider joining their little operation; they thought right, it was not illegal just a bit devious, and I needed the money.

First port of call was my old friend the nightclub manager, when the facts and figures were explained to him he was, unsurprisingly, more than keen to play ball. The dray would deliver his order, with ours included, he'd ring us up and we would whip round for our portion and pay him cash; he was making excellent money every week without even lifting a finger.

Everything was running smoothly, we moved into a new warehouse in Plymouth and business was brisk, the only problem was getting enough Courage Best Bitter at the right price. We managed to convince the nightclub manager to tell his sales rep that he wanted to try 'real ale' in his back bar and, although it sounded highly suspicious when no other nightclub in the country sold real ale, they duly fitted a beer engine and began delivering the beer. We began ordering in relatively low quantities and gradually kept stepping it up. I don't know how the manager kept a straight face when he told the rep it was selling like hot cakes because the beer pump was never even connected to a barrel. Finally, the brewery realised they were being duped and it was costing them dearly: for every barrel that went into the club at high discounts they were losing a barrel in a tied pub on which they were giving no discount, and we were living high on the difference. The area manager went to the club and explained that with only one beer engine, even if it was being pulled non-stop every night, it could not shift the amount of ale that had been ordered: our little game was up. Not to worry, there were plenty more opportunities to be had and that little operation is now well established and totally legitimate; well, almost!

It was fun for a while, but when a local brewery took out a court injunction to prevent me going into any of their pubs I felt it was a good time to move on again. I thought I'd buy a bar in Spain and went over for a couple of weeks to see what was available, which entailed viewing many of the properties in question and drinking with a few of the proprietors to get the full story. I learned that I could not raise enough money for a decent business and buying a small bar would have meant working twenty odd hours a day just to survive. I also learned that too many San Miguels gave me a dreadful hangover, and the temptation to imbibe when working all those hours in the heat would have been too much for me to handle on a daily basis. At least I was able to be honest with myself, so I came back to England and bought a café, even though I'd never felt a burning desire to binge on bacon sandwiches or tea.

The business itself was good and the staff were always ready for a laugh. If it hadn't been for the customers it would have been an ideal way to spend a year or so. I'm easy going, eat what I'm given, and very seldom complain so I had no idea what a moaning bunch of whingers the general public can be when it comes to food: they'd order breakfast then give specific instructions about how they wanted each item cooked. The bacon crispy but not the sausage, egg turned, toast only lightly browned, coffee hot but not too hot; they must have thought they were at the Savoy Grill not a 'greasy spoon' in a shopping precinct on a council estate! At night the local lads would congregate, drink strong lager and fool around, kicking balls and generally acting like louts. It was only a matter of time before shop windows started to get broken but the police were, as usual in these circumstances, unable or unwilling to sort the matter: some line about their hands being tied, human rights and so on. One evening I got a call from a girl who worked in the café and lived in a flat in the precinct, informing me that my window had just been smashed. I threw Murphy in the back of the car and tore up there to find about fifteen or twenty youths standing around. They must have heard me screech into the car park; I grabbed Murphy, ran straight up to them and, through gritted teeth, asked which of the louts had done it; it was plain to see I did not intend to have a discussion with the culprit and so, understandably, none of them were prepared to admit guilt. I called the police who said, unsurprisingly, there was nothing they could do, not even about the underage drinking. I asked what would have happened if I had walloped one of them and was advised I would have been charged with assault: the lunatics had finally taken over the asylum. There was one parting piece of advice before they left: had I ever considered installing CCTV? I wondered whether they had ever considered why nobody has faith in the police anymore.

I sold the café and was glad to get rid of it, joined a local gym and started training again. After a couple of months I bumped into the regional sales manager for Bass and we got chatting. Two weeks later I was back in the beer trade selling for Bass again, trying to make amends for all the business I'd taken off them when I was with Courage. I stuck at it for a couple of years but times were changing fast and I felt old: I was only forty four but it was all laptop computers and university graduates. I decided it was time to terminate my love affair with the brewing industry and seek pastures new and I sent my resignation by first-class post although, in retrospect, I probably should have emailed it, that's how outdated I was! Now for something completely different: but what?

Success is a journey, not a destination.

Bruce Lee

15
The wonderful world of finance

I found it exhilarating to be walking away from the drinks industry in much the same way as I had when I left the navy. I had a multitude of happy memories and a belief that I had been privileged to have been so well rewarded for doing something I enjoyed, matched by the conviction that change was in the air and it was the right time to move on. Change is inevitable but sometimes the speed of these changes can be difficult to come to terms with; I know from colleagues still at sea how drastically the British Merchant Navy has altered over the years, in the early 60's there were over 2,000 ships proudly flying the Red Ensign, now there are less than 200 and the vast majority of those are probably manned by foreign crews. It's the same story in the brewing industry, when I started in the early 80's there were 'the big six' breweries, names like Courage, Bass, Whitbread and Watneys had been around for two hundred years or more and were visible on every high street; not any more, they have long since been swallowed up by foreign conglomerates.

This acceptance that I had to seek pastures new lifted a weight off my shoulders and gave me a new found freedom to start afresh. Exactly what I was going to start was not so clear but this was hardly new territory for me and there was no sense of panic, although in retrospect, maybe there should have been.

Britannic Assurance had just advertised in the local newspaper for trainee financial advisers, they offered full training and a reasonable salary while studying; it had to be worth a try even though I had no idea what a financial adviser actually did. I remember the interview well, first they gave me a simple test, which was embarrassingly easy, and then I was grilled by the branch manager as to my suitability for the position. It is my experience that a lot of interviewers set out to intimidate the candidates; I was never sure if this was because they felt in a position of power or if it was a cover for their own insecurity; probably both. Whatever the reason, I always performed better when the interviewer was relaxed and genuine; if they tried to intimidate me it was like a red rag to a bull. At one meeting, the interviewer put a pen into my hand and told me to sell it to him. I was sorely tempted to suggest that he shove it up his clacker but instead, simply pointed out the benefits of the object in question, as was expected of me, like some sort of performing monkey. I could never work for such a complete plonker. At Britannic the branch manager was in full swing: he had given me the story of how he had joined the company straight from university and worked his way up. I was doing my best to look suitably impressed but it was not easy, and then he threw me a question which was designed to make me flounder: "You have always sold tangible products, something you can see and feel, what makes you so sure you could sell pension and insurance products which have no immediate feel good factor for the client, and whose benefits may not be realised for many years, if ever?" He then sank back into his chair expecting to observe me as I struggled to justify why he should employ me. It was a perfectly valid question and I was finding it difficult to think of a good answer, so I turned it back to him, "I don't have enough knowledge of your industry to answer that, but you can see from the sales figures in front of you that I have had considerable success with various companies over many years, and have no reason to doubt my ability to sell your products; what specific concerns do you have that suggest I couldn't?" I did not mean my answer to sound flippant but I could not accept that selling this stuff was rocket science; anyway, the other candidates could not have been up to much because I got the job.

The following week I was sent on a five week residential course at their training centre in Birmingham; apparently I had to be in possession of a Full Financial Planning Certificate to qualify as a financial adviser, and this consisted of three exams which all had to be passed individually. Although it was originally envisaged that candidates would have two years to study for them, we had been chosen to be fast tracked, taking the first exam after two weeks, the second two weeks later, and the final one the following week. Before I left Plymouth I had been given two books which I had presumed were reference books, and to find out that I had to absorb all the facts and figures contained within them came as something of a major shock; if I failed the exams I would be out of a job.

The following five weeks entailed the most intensive period of study I have ever undertaken. The products were all totally new to me and the majority I had never even heard of; I had facts and figures turning over in my mind and didn't know if I was coming or going. Despite all this, I passed, so after five weeks I was a fully qualified financial adviser which, when you stop to consider the implications, is a frightening thought. I was reminded of the spoof advert, 'six months ago I couldn't spell teacher, now I are one!'

I need not have worried that I was going to give anybody the wrong advice about how to invest their money because when I returned to Plymouth and was given my area, I quickly tumbled that no-one within that area had any money to invest. My territory was entirely made up of council estates, not ordinary council estates but those where, if you leave your car for longer than it takes to post a letter, you count yourself lucky if you have any wheels left when you return. The general idea was that I spend the mornings collecting premiums of between one and two pounds from my customers and try to get an appointment to review their finances, jargon for 'sell them something', or get them to refer me on to family and friends so I could sell them something. That may have been the idea but many could not even afford the premiums on their existing policies, some would hide when I rang the doorbell and I often considered carrying an adjustable spanner to help wrench the money out of their clenched fists. If I ever did get to sit in front of anybody it was essential that I establish how much money they had left over at the end of the month in order to advise them what to do with it; invariably they had nothing left or were in debt and needed a loan. This was not going to plan. People of a certain age will remember the ubiquitous 'Man from the Pru' who was always shown on the television calling round to see his band of merry customers, well I had become the poor man's equivalent, "The Tit from the Brit!"

The company decided to send me on a variety of courses to ensure I had a thorough understanding of their products, and these courses were invariably run by an independent team of former financial advisers who often had an inflated opinion of themselves. They were usually a good laugh as long as you didn't take them too seriously and I recall one incident which still makes me smile. First thing Monday morning the course tutor stood at the front and introduced himself in a manner implying that he was not a chap to be messed with which suggested that everyone else had already messed with him and he was frightened it was going to happen again; he obviously felt attack would be his best form of defence.

He explained a basic sales technique of asking 'open' questions, which are questions where the recipient cannot just answer 'yes' or 'no' but has to give out some information. Our first exercise of the day would entail splitting us into groups of three for ten minutes, one asking open questions to the other and the third acting as an observer, to ensure we fully understood the concept. I was instructed to be the one asking the questions and so, along with two colleagues, went out into the bar to get some privacy. To be honest we all just introduced ourselves to each other and had a general chat about where we came from before we filed back in and sat down. The tutor started with the first man, "Well, what did you find out?" and the man duly responded with a bit of information about his teammate, but this was not enough for the tutor who demanded more, "And?...Is that all you got?" I was up next, what had I established? "Well" I said in a positive tone, "His name is Paul, he's from Swansea and he's a keen golfer." "And?" The tutor said in an expectant tone. I added a bit more waffle to try and satisfy him. "And?" he replied in a tone that was meant to convey a level of disappointment. If this fellow wanted to play silly buggers I was more than happy to oblige, so off I went, "He had played golf for Wales and represented them in numerous competitions!" "And?" "He loves fishing." "Sea or freshwater?" "Sea fishing, in fact shark fishing to be more exact!" Now, of course I was making all this up as we went along, so I could have kept going all day. My two colleagues thought I had gone completely mad, but the funny thing was that the shark fishing story genuinely interested the tutor and he began asking serious questions. "Shark fishing in England?" "Oh yes, he goes to Looe in Cornwall, which is the headquarters of the U.K. shark fishing association!" "What type of sharks does he catch?" At this point I was pissing myself and thought I'd call my colleague's bluff, so I said "I don't know, we ran out of time, you'll have to ask him that!"

I thought my game was up and I was going to be hung out to dry, but Paul just picked up the baton and kept on running with it, even going into great detail about the different baits he used, and then he told a story of how once, in a small boat off Portugal, a hammerhead shark came right alongside and let him stroke it! It was pure Monty Python and the tutor lapped it up. Eventually we moved onto the next three, then at coffee break, when the rest of the class found out we had been making it up as we went along, it meant the tutor was the only one not in on the joke; he was the joke.

Once all the courses had finished, and the reality of the job had sunk in, I felt I had been more than a little misled as regards the potential to earn money in my assigned area. Everybody in the office was so concerned with their own activities that I was pretty much left to get on with things myself, which is fine when you know what you should be doing, but not otherwise. I once asked my manager for some advice and he suggested knocking on doors and trying to sell children's savings plans. I had a better idea and contacted a recruitment agency who promptly fixed me up with a much improved position. My misgivings were confirmed within a couple of years when the Britannic closed its regional offices and laid off its entire sales staff.

Every now and then I have come across some exceptional salesmen, and in a world of mediocrity, they are a pleasure to watch. They usually have quite a disarming manner which encourages a bond of trust, and before you know what has happened you have divulged personal information to someone who is essentially a total stranger, and who will then proceed to use that information to sell you something. When that talent is allied with the tenacity of a dog with a bone, success is assured. Chris was one such character, an ex-Navy helicopter pilot. He interviewed me over coffee in a motel lounge, cut through all the usual preliminaries of these meetings and got straight to the point; this was exactly how I liked to operate and I lay all my cards on the table. He suggested that as I had only been in finance for eight months it might be difficult to secure a position but, despite this, he still offered me some sound advice as to how I could improve my performance and for that I was most grateful.

I felt the interview had gone well but was not overly optimistic. That evening Chris rang me from Taunton, he was with the regional director and they wanted to see me immediately; we met in Exeter within the hour. Despite my lack of financial experience they were prepared to gamble that my enthusiasm and sales skills would overcome this difficulty. The gamble paid off for all of us: in my first month I earned four thousand pounds, and within two months I was in the top ten of the company performers.

Chris was a first class manager, he guided, encouraged and nurtured; I can never recall him criticising or belittling anybody who was trying their best and we had a mutual respect for each other. He went on to become the Managing Director of a finance company and tried to recruit me a few years ago; in retrospect, I should have accepted the offer.

After a year I secured a position with a national equity release company, I made an instant impact and in the three years

I was with them was consistently the highest performer. I found the job effortless but the company was growing rapidly and always looking for ways to maximise their profits, and there was nothing wrong with that until they hit on what they considered to be the jackpot. I won't complicate the story with all the details but suffice to say that their scheme involved elderly homeowners selling their homes and reinvesting the money they did not immediately need into bonds and insurance products, all of which paid handsome commissions. It was an obscenely manipulative scheme in which the clients were needlessly exposed to the considerable risk of losing everything and I was not prepared to play any part in this cruel deception. The pressure came from above that this was to be company policy and I had to accept it or leave, so I left. I heard some time later that the Financial Services Authority also thought it stank and went through the company like a dose of salts. I have a wry smile to myself whenever I hear the company director speaking in the media about how important it is to look after the elderly and ensure they get the best advice because I possess an email which clearly shows how devious he was prepared to be in order to increase profits. The fact that the vast majority of the sales force was prepared to sell these plans rather than lose their jobs gives a good insight into society today; no doubt they based their decision on the Nuremberg Defence, "We were only obeying orders!" What it did for their consciences only they would know, but from my perspective, I sleep quite soundly.

I was out of work again and despite my age still felt sufficiently confident to reply to an advert placed in the national press by a mortgage company offering a very attractive package, excellent remuneration and company car: it had to be worth a try. On my first day, I was given the keys to a Rover 75 and an agenda for a two week course; the company operated solely in the sub-prime market which can be very profitable, if a trifle risky, as we all now know. The first week was spent learning about the implications of County Court Judgments and bankruptcy orders, but by the second week the full implications of their modus operandi became clear, and it was not a pretty sight. To put it simply, the company bought mailing lists of people with financial difficulties, and these people were then contacted by a well trained and highly motivated telesales team who were handsomely rewarded for making appointments. Many of those contacted wanted to increase their level of borrowing but, because of their poor credit history, were not welcomed by mainstream lenders; the company exploited this to their advantage. Despite the undeniable fact that most were having difficulty repaying their existing loans, it was deemed acceptable to increase their debt and, as it was now sub-prime, charge a considerably higher interest rate. This in itself should have raised serious concerns but, as an encore, they were then pressurised to take out a form of insurance called 'lump sum mortgage protection', a highly contentious product at the best of times and the cost of which usually ran into thousands of pounds that was promptly added to their loan. Now you don't need to be Einstein to see that this piece of grotesque financial wizardry takes blatantly unfair advantage of a vulnerable section of society and could seldom, if ever, be construed as offering anybody best advice. Recommending that someone in a precarious financial position should dramatically increase their loan at a considerably higher rate of interest would appear to be stupid. However, the owner of this company was not stupid; he was greedy and obnoxious, but not stupid. He had a lawyer who looked almost Dickensian with his crumpled suit, scruffy hair and horn rimmed glasses, and who ensured everything was 'street legal'. The clients had to sign so many documents that when the proverbial shit hit the fan, there was no way they could say they had not been told all the facts and, as if that were not enough, the whole meeting was taped from start to finish.

When I questioned the need for all this documentation and taping I was informed by the lawyer that I would do as I was told, or else. It was the 'or else' bit that found me an hour later with my bags packed standing on the platform waiting for a train back to Plymouth, out of work again, but I did have a fallback position. Not ideal I had to admit, but beggars can't be choosers.

My office at the back of the estate agency felt like a prison. I had been offered the position of mortgage adviser based on my previous sales figures, and the company had high expectations of me but the reality was that I had never actually completed a normal mortgage before, only lifetime mortgages; not even a distant relative. A senior adviser based a few miles away in the main branch was available on the phone to offer assistance if I needed it, and I needed it a great deal in the first few days; I felt lost in a maze of 'buy to lets', 'let to buys' and 'income multiples'. Although I found selling easy, in the first couple of months I sold more than the other two advisers combined, the paperwork was a tedious stream of form after form after form. The rest of the team were a pleasure to work with but I found that being tied to my office from eight in the morning until gone six at night was not an easy readjustment after more than twenty years on the road. Often I would sit all day with nothing to do, itching to get out; I was used to chasing business not waiting for it to find me, and the time just dragged. I offered to work on a part time basis for a reduced salary, confident that my commissions would not suffer, but this was not company policy and that was ruled out. Finally, after eight months of this daily grind, the boredom got the better of me and I did what I do best: I left.

I took a month out and went for an advanced scuba diving qualification; it seemed a good idea at the time but was a lot of bother just to see a few dogfish and the odd lobster at the bottom of Plymouth Sound. Suitably refreshed, it was time to check out the situations vacant pages again. A local soft drinks company wanted a salesman, though at fifty years old I was applying more in hope than anticipation, but I'm never one to entirely rule out hope and the following week I was learning all about the finer points of making cola and lemonade. The job itself was OK but it was very much a one man show and his management style was unorthodox in the extreme. My heart wasn't in it, and a year to the day after I walked into the office, I walked back out of it for good.

Brothers and sisters, I bid you beware, of giving your heart
to a dog to tear.
Rudyard Kipling

16
Dogged pursuits

I gave a lot of thought to considering what my next move
should be but could not find a clear course of action; I needed
something to motivate me, something to aim for, but it proved
to be elusive. I had no lingering desire to travel anywhere, I'd
been to all the places I especially wanted to visit and was quite
content to remain where I was; anyway, I was loathe to leave my
dogs. Unfortunately, this settled state did not mean I was entirely
happy with my lot, merely that I could think of nothing which
would particularly improve it. However, I still needed to earn a
living, and was not smitten with the prospect of menial work
stacking shelves on the night shift at Asda.

As people approach middle age they tend to reflect on their
lives and ponder their achievements or, as is more often the case,
their failures. It is distressing to regret those things not
accomplished but I believe it is the realisation that it is too late to
make amends that often underlies the despondency of the mid-
life crisis. I always seemed to lack the ambition and bum kissing
required when climbing the slippery ladder of promotion in
pursuit of success; perhaps this was a result of viewing
relationships, both personal and professional, as only temporary
in nature. I saw no advantage to settling down, surely much
better to just enjoy the ride and when the good times come to an
end, as undoubtedly they must, move on. No stress, worry or
sleepless nights wondering if the boss was going to be in a good
mood because the worst he could do was sack me, and I was
probably thinking of leaving anyway. It was liberating being
beholden to no one but it had its drawbacks too: unemployment

for example!

While I mulled over the options on the table, sign on the dole or stack shelves, I was approached by somebody I had worked with in the past who needed a partner for financial sales and marketing; it was on a small scale but sufficiently viable to put the spectre of a trolley load of beans on the back burner for a while.

That little enterprise worked well for a few years, until a combination of the 'Credit Crunch' and the collapse of a local publication, which was our main source of revenue, brought it to an end. Always trying to find a positive side to events, at least it gave me some time to pursue my enduring passion in life: dogs.

Having owned a pair of Rottweilers I felt quite confident in my ability to handle dogs. While Guinness had proved her mettle in the pub, Murphy was such a size he never felt the need to prove anything, although in reality he was a big softie. His size, however, did cause a few problems: he broke three windows by jumping against them before we decided that double glazing was a necessity, and as we had two young boys it was not unusual for him to turn around and inadvertently propel one of them across the room with his back end, but there was no malice in it and he was never vicious.

I recall hiking and camping overnight on Dartmoor in December; it was bitterly cold and snow was falling. Murphy wasn't bothered in the slightest, he swam across the rivers and would have happily walked all night. After we had set up the tent and had something to eat we were not long in getting our heads down. In the early hours of the morning I was woken by my friend, an ex-marine, struggling to get Murphy off him. He was tucked down into his sleeping bag and Murphy, ten stone if he was a pound, had rolled onto him trapping his arms and was snoring away contentedly. My English bull terrier was snuggled down in my sleeping bag keeping my feet warm. The next day was a bit embarrassing as an ex-marine and an ex-navigator got lost; at least we could take comfort in the old adage that there are two types of people who walk on Dartmoor: those who have been lost at least once and liars. At times like these you need a gut instinct and I followed mine unerringly: within a couple of hours we were snug in the Warren House Inn quaffing fine ale and warming ourselves in front of the famous fire that never goes out.

Warren House Inn, Dartmoor (Steve Waite).

Being the owner of an old Rottweiler and a young bull terrier, the logical course of action was to breed a litter from Duchess and keep a dog to replace the ageing Murphy; it made perfect sense to me, although I can't deny that my wife did not share my enthusiasm, even more so when I told her that I planned to use the kitchen as the whelping room. On the appropriate day, I took Duchess to a stud dog near London but with a disappointing result. Although all my dogs get plenty of exercise, most kennel dogs do not enjoy the same level of fitness; the stud dog was run ragged after ten minutes and in no state to perform his duties. Same outcome the next day, but at least she'd made a new friend. Six months later when she came into season again I took her to her original breeder to use one of his stud dogs. This time it was a clinical procedure and I felt a bit uncomfortable with it; I didn't expect her to be given a bunch of roses or box of chocolates but thought a quick lick of the ear might have been appreciated: it was not to be.

Nine weeks later and out popped a lone puppy, and a bitch at that, not exactly the result I had planned. It is well known that it is often problematic to keep two dogs of the same size and sex in certain breed types; it may be fine with Labradors but is not generally considered wise with bull terriers, however, there is always the exception to the rule and it was my intention to prove it. I named the pup Dolly and she was a beauty. Going for walks could be tricky; if they all saw a cat before I did I was in serious danger of pirouetting and getting screwed into the ground, but on the plus side I was never worried about getting mugged.

As Dolly began to mature she started to fight with her mother, the encounters getting ever more vicious as they became more evenly contested; both dogs got on well with Murphy and were no problems at all individually, but they refused to accept each other and I could see no end to this conundrum. A well known characteristic of bull terriers is their ability to lock on and hold tight, an admirable quality when pitted against a bull but a damned nuisance when it is one of your pets on the receiving end. The crunch came one day when they decided to have a go at each other and I had my arm ripped open trying to part them; I went to hospital and Dolly went to the in-laws. It broke my heart but I had no option, she lived the life of a madam for the next twelve years and had my in-laws wrapped around her paw.

A couple of years later I suggested to the in-laws that their lives would be considerably enriched by letting Dolly have a litter and, surprisingly, they were more than happy with the idea. I chose a handsome show winner for her and after a successful mating she produced six beautiful puppies. I drove up to Bristol to check the litter and ensure everything was in order before leaving my mother-in-law to spend the next five weeks cleaning up their calling cards.

I kept one of the puppies, pure white with two black ears, and called him Delboy; he was the softest dog I ever owned and even loved cats. I had a modicum of success showing him but I never really took to dog shows per se. I remember driving into the car park for the West of England Bull Terrier Club show, Delboy was curled up asleep but Duchess, whom I had only taken because she didn't like to be left out, was sitting up looking out of the window. She had one ear hanging down and scars on her face from relentlessly chasing squirrels through gorse bushes; the other exhibitors no doubt thought I was being outrageously optimistic by entering her so were shocked when Delboy jumped out and proudly swaggered his way to second place.

Murphy went into rapid decline after reaching eleven; it was heartbreaking watching such a giant of a dog fade away. I still remember an incident when he was only about a year old and almost overnight he became very aggressive with other dogs whenever he was on a lead; he was fine off the lead but once on it he became a different dog and a Rottweiler in full voice is something to behold. I went to a dog training class to seek some advice and was told in no uncertain terms that castration was the only answer, which seemed a somewhat draconian measure for a little excessive barking. I was advised by the vet that it was possible to get an injection that would simulate the effects of castration before committing to surgery and this seemed a logical road to go down before taking an irreversible step. I'm glad I did because he changed from a lively dog to an old man before my very eyes which was not what I wanted at all. As it was, he soon calmed down anyway once he had grown out of his juvenile delinquency and the problem solved itself; I have nothing against castration and would still consider it under certain circumstances, but it is not a silver bullet for all canine behavioural problems.

After Murphy had passed on, life was comparatively easy with just a pair of dogs but it is never totally stress free with bull terriers around. They were originally bred to fight and the trait is always present; with Delboy it was buried so deep that I never even heard him growl, but Duchess was an altogether different proposition: if a strange dog ever started on her it was immediately shown the error of its ways and never made the mistake again.

As Duchess went into her twelfth year I could see the end was not far away, and then I lost Delboy to an illness that nobody could really explain, despite paying huge fees to specialists in my desperate attempts to find a cure. Every dog owner would understand my emotions at that time and it is in those moments that you ask yourself why you ever took on a dog when you know the pain it will ultimately cause; these have always been the darkest periods in my life and the memories never fade.

We had decided that we would not get another bully but instead go for something less intimidating. Fate intervened when I bumped into a lady who I knew resettled rescued bull terriers. She was walking one at the time and I offered to take it up on the moors with my sons and run off some of its excess energy. She jumped at the chance. When she came round that night to collect him he was curled up fast asleep on the sofa; I enquired about her plans for him and, when she said she was desperate to find him a new home, I glanced over at the dog, and then my wife; it was not a difficult decision. We called him Bud and he won our hearts.

I used to run the dogs in a large field by a river, Bud would be like a cork out of a bottle and Duchess would wander along at her own pace. One sunny afternoon, Bud came running over carrying a long branch in his jaws that he had pulled out of the river and Duchess grabbed the other end as if she were a puppy again. They tugged and growled and played for a while but as I started to make my way back to the car Duchess lay down on the grass and looked at me. I knew straight away that this was the end, her whole demeanour was totally focused on me and as I sat next to her, cradling her head and talking to her, she slipped away. I was devastated. I picked her up and carried her back in my arms, reminiscent of the time one January when she broke her leg on Dartmoor and I had to carry her a mile through the snow, but this time there was to be no happy ending.

For a few years we just had Bud which made life easier with two young lads as well, but as the boys grew up and no longer wanted to be seen out with mum and dad, my mind began to wander about which breed I would get next. I had just read a book written by Robert Kaleski in 1914; he was one of the most respected dog men in Australia at that time and had established the breed standard for the Australian cattle dog back in 1903. He wrote from experience, as somebody who had bred and worked this rugged breed for many years and wanted to ensure their purity of lines would be maintained for future generations. In the early days of the colony, the settlers had brought collies with them to work the cattle over the vast expanses of land but found that the conditions were too harsh for them, so to remedy this they crossed them with the Australian dingo with considerable success. He once wrote, "Nothing in the bush makes as good a mate as a cattle dog. Besides working cattle he is a great fighter, a good game dog, a retriever and the finest watchdog possible." It conjures up an image of the stockman and his herd blazing a trail through the outback with his trusty 'Bluey', keeping the cattle on the move in the heat and dust of the day. All very adventurous, of course, but a long way from the rain and damp of a Devon winter where mine would be calling home; more research was needed.

I learned from the internet that they needed a lot of exercise and that seemed to fit ideally with my lifestyle as I love walking over the moors. They are not a large dog and usually resemble a small, thick-set, blue dingo in appearance, another plus as there was less chance of ending up on my backside if it decided to chase something. They are, I learned, naturally suspicious of strangers, yet another bonus as I was hoping it might keep the mother-in-law away. Homework completed, I made the decision to get a cattle dog.

They are quite a rare breed and I had to wait a few months before I secured one. I drove to Lincoln to pick up the pup but, as it was a six hundred mile round trip, I had chosen to book into a motel and collect the dog the following morning. That evening, I went to a local pub for a bite to eat and a nightcap and, as often happens, I got to chatting with a small number of the locals. In the convivial atmosphere I ended up drinking more than intended and arrived at the breeders next morning feeling slightly the worse for wear but eager to pick up my new pup and be on my way. It was chaos: there were pups running everywhere, hanging off my laces and disappearing behind the furniture. I made my choice and as we were doing the paperwork I saw my treasured puppy hanging precariously from the arms of the breeder's three year old son. Imagining visions of a broken leg I persuaded him to part with his toy and ended up signing the papers with a wriggling, squealing bundle of fur between my legs.

Having successfully got the pup into the travelling crate in the back of the car, I started on my way home but hadn't even got out of the gate before she started yapping in such a high pitched tone that I half expected the windscreen to shatter; it was horrendous. I figured she would soon calm down but within five minutes the noise was accompanied by an odour familiar to dog owners; this was not good. I pulled over at the first available spot and climbed into the back to try and clean her up and calm her down; the prospect of three hundred miles of this was not something I had anticipated at all and the hangover was not helping matters. I stopped for some essential supplies, Anadin Extra and water, then put my foot down to get the ordeal over as fast as possible, and she finally went to sleep. I prayed there would be no hold ups on the motorway.

Once home, I let her have a little run in the garden and introduced her to Bud, taking great care to ensure he realised it was not a toy to be eaten. Poor Bud was getting old and had heart problems but still wanted to play, he could no longer get up the stairs and used to sleep on the sofa but the pup didn't know any of this and was always trying to jump on him. Old dogs seem to have an understanding with pups and Bud put up with her for a year before the end finally came; it was his time and it comes to us all eventually, but it never gets any easier. He was a sad loss.

We called her Bundy after the famous Australian rum and she grew into a delightful dog, a pleasure to own. The first inkling of trouble ahead came one day when she was out in the garden. Her ever alert ears picked up a noise a couple of gardens down, and like a champion hurdler she hopped over the four and a half foot fence, took a few strides and went over the next as well. Realising how easy it was, she would hop over at the slightest sound, sniff around and hop back, you couldn't even put her out for a pee without the prospect of another feat of athleticism. I had to put up six foot fencing as a matter of urgency which she initially viewed as an exciting challenge and she still has the occasional attempt at that height even now.

It seemed a good idea to have a litter out of her and keep a dog; this would be my final challenge in the canine arena so I chose what I considered to be the best stud dog in the country. Unfortunately, I was not the only one to appreciate him, and the month before Bundy came into season he was sold to a breeder in the USA and went on to become a champion over there as well. The best available option was his son, so I approached the owner with what many would consider a foolish request: I felt uncomfortable with the normal mating procedure as it was so unnatural and wondered if the owner would be happy to let the dogs run free and see if nature took its course. They agreed, and I took Bundy up for a week of passion.

The mating was a success and produced six beautiful pups; I kept one and called him Breaker. One of the advantages of their unusual coat is that the true blue colour is supposed to make them virtually invisible in the dark, which is ideal for stalking cattle near Alice Springs in the dead of night but a bloody nightmare early on misty winter mornings down the local woods: I can hear them barking away but haven't got a clue where they are. They are, without question, the most challenging breed I have had the pleasure to own, but I could not imagine life without them!

"Where's the beef?" Bundy (L), Breaker, Whitsand Bay, Cornwall, 2011.

There is only 'what is'. The 'what-should-be' never did exist, but people keep trying to live up to it. There is only 'what is'!
Lenny Bruce

17
In the end, there is only the end

I appreciate that much of my behaviour will appear selfish and thoughtless to many but before passing judgement, I suggest people spend a few minutes reflecting on their own lives and the consequences of their actions. For as long as I can remember I have struggled with crucial aspects of authority, and although there are many people that I hold in high regard, my respect is reserved for the person not the position. When I was young I was taught to respect my elders, but could see nothing deserving of this deference solely because someone had managed to stay alive. This attitude ensured I was classified as a troublemaker from as early as primary school and led some teachers to believe it was their duty to break me. Ironically, it was a simple case of cause and effect: if a teacher respected me then I would respond accordingly, but if they set out to intimidate me then the result was contemptuous indifference. Respect can never be garnered through fear; obedience perhaps, but never respect.

This became the pattern of my life: as a human version of Marmite, people either loved me or hated me. I like to think there were more of the former than the latter, but that was perhaps not the case in my formative years. There was one teacher who kept in touch for years after I'd joined the navy, while others felt I should have been expelled for my behaviour. The same was true at sea where some officers considered I was an asset and appreciated having me on their watch as it eased the workload, while those who attempted to stamp their authority invariably regarded me as lazy and incompetent.

One of the best examples of this was aboard the S.S.

Hadriania. The Mate was outstanding, he encouraged me and I learned a great deal from him, and in return I worked exceptionally hard; it was my last trip as a cadet and he felt confident enough in my abilities to trust me with much of the work he was expected to do, leaving him free to catch up on numerous other tasks. There is no doubt I was a considerable benefit to him, we got along famously and I thoroughly enjoyed working with him; he recommended me for promotion and many years later I was a guest at his home. This was in stark contrast to the Second Mate, who was full of his own self importance and considered my usual irreverent and jocular manner to be a slight on his authority. He treated me like a lackey and was rewarded with the laziest and most elusive cadet imaginable; the more he blustered, the more I baited him. In desperation, he went to the Mate to complain about my incompetence but to no effect because the Mate knew it was a result of his poor management style. Two men, same ship, and two totally different outcomes: one earned my respect and as a consequence, hard work and loyalty, the other demanded it and got nothing but contempt.

This is just a small personal example within the framework of a wider society that demands respect for its institutions, the processes by which those institutions function and those individuals who hold executive power, many of whom, on closer inspection, do not deserve it. When the surface is scratched we find institutions that historically have been held in high esteem but are, as often as not, rotten to the core, and a betrayal of trust that can be hard to comprehend. It seems that the processes and criteria we use for selecting our leaders and their cronies may be flawed. I once felt isolated and alone in my disdain for these people, processes and institutions but in recent years the general public has been presented with such a generous serving of a tasteless stew of thieving, cheating, greed and corruption washed down with thinly disguised lies that they have slowly but inexorably become aware of what has been going on. We have been shafted for so long now that these revelations are no longer just embarrassing, but a damning indictment of a system that favours the few while failing the many. We have only one world and we're sharing it with billions of other people, all of whom have similar needs to our own. If we fail to accept that reality, then we will be forced to accept the consequences. We seem to have developed a system that increasingly applauds and rewards self-interest, greed, arrogance, bare-faced mendacity, ignorance, hubris, aggressive petulance, self-importance, selfish myopia and, paradoxically, even remunerates the almost inevitable failure that results from these traits. It is a system that often encourages the overindulgence of the overrated, corruption, incompetence, fraud, laziness, lack of responsibility, lack of accountability, lack of perspective and a widespread disregard, and even contempt, for the impact of our actions on others, while actively discouraging and penalising independent thought and action, painstaking attention to detail, any challenge to the status quo, and the whistleblowers who risk their jobs, pensions and freedom by exposing these failings.

Bankers feel they have been unfairly treated, but even their own regulatory body, the Financial Services Authority, has become a laughing stock for its ineptitude; with so many mis-selling scandals you have to ask if anybody had a clue what was going on. Whether by accident or design, it has been suggested that the revolving door between financial institutions and regulators permitted the greatest robbery in human history: never was so much owed to so many by so few.

This ludicrous litany revealed an ongoing assault on common sense. "The Pensions Scandal", where clients were advised to shift from 'gold-plated' company pension schemes into high risk investments, very profitable but shocking advice that resulted in millions paid in compensation. Then there were the Mortgage Endowments that couldn't pay off the mortgages, and more millions in compensation. In 2011, banks had to repay further millions in mis-sold Payment Protection Insurance; you don't need to be a genius to see a common thread: if there's money to be made regardless of the means, rest assured they will try.

Certain aspects of the industry seemed like an accident waiting to happen, like a massive financial farce starring Botchit, Grabbit & Runne Property Consultancy. Devising a scheme to allow first-time homebuyers, with no previous experience of the expense of running a household, to borrow 125% of the value of their property requires careful consideration of the risks. The most obvious risk might be that should house prices fall, a normal part of cyclical market fluctuation, then the lender would have a large amount of money unsecured and, therefore, at risk. Should the borrower suffer any financial setback at all, for example unemployment, sickness or divorce, all entirely possible, then financial meltdown would be almost inevitable. Individuals with a sense of responsibility might be expected to carefully and cogently consider these matters before dismissing such a scheme, but not the board of Northern Rock. When, as a direct result of this decision, the bank collapsed and had to be bailed out by taxpayers, the cost was horrendous. The bank was split into two parts: the 'good' part, which sold recently at an estimated loss to the tax payer of about £500million, and the 'bad' part, which still owes the Treasury around £21billion. Although the full potential losses are unclear, they will almost certainly be dire! So, did the mastermind behind this piece of financial brilliance fall on his sword? Not a bit of it. With head and two fingers held high he sauntered off smiling at the prospect of picking up his pension, reportedly £305,000 a year when he reaches 60!

Fred Goodwin also deserves recognition for his role in the Royal Bank of Scotland (RBS) debacle. In February 2009, RBS announced the greatest loss in UK corporate history. The reported figures are mind boggling. Apparently, their 2008 losses totalled over £24billion and they held around £325billion worth of 'toxic assets', figures that are so staggeringly large it is hard to fully appreciate the enormity of such a remarkable result. To date, the government has pumped £45billion into RBS, a sum that might be better viewed as a generous donation to the social welfare of a small but significant part of society. For his role in this historic achievement, the former chief executive reportedly walked away with a pension of £342,500 a year and a lump sum of £2.7million, on which RBS, or more correctly the taxpayer, had generously paid his tax. And to add insult to injury, he 'earned', though perhaps not the most appropriate use of that word, a bonus of £2.86million, apparently for what may best be described as an unforgettable performance in "The Largest Corporate Loss in UK History". It's a blockbusting saga that will be playing throughout the land for many years to come. His two-finger salute to the taxpayer was right up there with Adam Applegarth of Northern Rock. It is interesting to note that Mr Applegarth is now at the U.S. private equity firm, Apollo, as senior adviser on the European fund that invests in distressed loans, a position for which he is indisputably well qualified! Recently, Sir Fred has been stripped of his knighthood and is now just plain old Fred Goodwin again, a decision which one leading financial publication lamented as "a whiff of rough justice here, other titled bankers who messed up have not lost their honours!" Using similar reasoning, perhaps it would not be fair to prosecute the looters who were caught in the London riots of 2011 because most rioters managed to escape unscathed.

In the current circumstances of widespread public anger, the recent spate of voluntary downgrading in the sizes of bank and public sector bonuses seems likely to be a temporary respite rather than any sort of fundamental and sustained reduction in the massive chasm that separates the salaries, bonuses, and offshore share options handed to the proponents of financial and commercial quackery, and the pittance so often paid to those who work at the sharp end of health, education, or local councils.

As a lifelong adherent of independent thought and action and associated non-compliance and disobedience, I believe that my admiration and respect is best reserved for those who earn it. As a consequence, I've been labelled a troublemaker for not simply accepting the wisdom and justice that is allegedly inherent in authority. In the light of recent events, I feel my scepticism has been well and truly vindicated.

I would be hard pressed to complete my story without

mentioning another pillar of the Establishment: the police. After so much scandal I think their credibility has already been significantly dented or worse: the Birmingham Six, the Bridgewater Three, and many other miscarriages of justice, so many in fact that there was enough material to keep the TV series "Rough Justice" busy for twenty five years.

One incident which reached the headlines was the death of Jean Charles de Menezes, an innocent young Brasilian who had seven bullets fired into his head at Stockwell tube station in 2005. It raises a lot of interesting questions about the way the police reacted in the aftermath of this tragedy. Tensions were understandably running high after the 7th July London bombings and in such circumstances accidents are a real risk. But covering up mistakes and playing fast and loose with the truth is another matter altogether.

When the investigation started into what went wrong and why, misleading statements came thick and fast. The logical first step was to investigate the CCTV footage, but according to a police report there was no footage due to a technical problem with the equipment. However, the Tube Lines consortium, who is responsible for maintaining the equipment, insisted that the cameras were in working order, and London Underground sources also insisted that at least three of the four cameras trained on the Stockwell tube platform were in full working order. Maybe the police had simply made an inadvertent mistake?

The police might have been on edge because, according to the information they gave to the pathologist, Menezes "vaulted over the ticket barriers and ran down the stairs of the tube station". But CCTV footage showed him calmly walking through the ticket barrier. Had the police inadvertently made another simple error?

When the deputy assistant commissioner Cressida Dick advised one of the surveillance officers that Menezes was *not* carrying anything that represented a security threat, you might have assumed the officer in question would have eased up a bit on his trigger finger, but it seems he preferred to ignore her and, instead, just deleted his computer notes which confirmed he had indeed received the message. Another day, another error, another mistake?

I wonder what would happen if I was arrested and made that many mistakes in my testimony, perhaps a charge of perverting the course of justice would be considered inevitable. It's difficult not to be cynical in the face of so much evidence, so perhaps my distrust of the police has not been unduly misdirected over the years: by comparison, even Clouseau looks clever.

A litany of errors or mistakes in the course of any day's work, whether intentional or otherwise, whether through greed, incompetence, malice, prejudice or crass stupidity, that leads to the punishment of the innocent and the failure to apprehend the guilty, should not be met with excuses, bonuses, apologies, promotions, complacency, apathetic acceptance or lengthy and carefully engineered enquiries designed to deliver smooth outcomes at some distant point in the future when the collective memory has faded, but with simple and instant dismissal. If you can't do the job properly, then for everyone's benefit, please, find yourself another. It's what most ordinary people on the planet have to put up with, so why not those in positions of power and privilege?

Another institution once considered to be worthy of respect was Parliament, the legislative seat of government, until the recent expenses scandal revealed that the majority of politicians seemed quite relaxed with their taxpayer-funded lifestyles. Some even had the gall to try and justify their extravagant claims, and it went right to the very top of both major parties. Even the Home Secretary was blatantly milking the system to an outrageous extent, claiming to live at her sister's house so she could abuse the second homes allowance. At least there is some consistency in this behaviour: as far back as Cromwell corruption was considered perfectly normal, so why would it be any different now. I have no personal grievance with these people but I find the hypocrisy difficult to digest. Laws may be made to be obeyed but, apparently, not by everyone.

Even in my short lifetime there have always been scandals, from the Profumo affair to Jeremy Thorpe to Sir John Major and Edwina Currie to Lord Prescott. It is no different in the USA, where the iconic JFK seemed to have a weakness for the ladies and even Hillary Clinton admitted that her husband, the President of the most powerful country in the world, "was a hard dog to keep on the porch!" These dalliances are just part of human nature, but when it comes to wars that cost people's lives it is a far more serious issue. The Iraq war saw one of the most contentious decisions ever taken by a British Government, and many accused Tony Blair of taking the country to war based on the now infamous 'Dodgy Dossier', which warned us that Saddam Hussein could have biological, chemical and nuclear weapons of mass destruction ready for use within forty five minutes. Precisely how many of these weapons did he have? Well, not quite none, but only a small quantity of aging chemicals and unusable munitions remained from 1991 although, like a mouldy sandwich from a Baghdad fridge, I'm not entirely dismissing the life-threatening potential of such hazards.

Tony Blair's actions were heavily influenced by his strident support for the USA. The same USA that advised the world that if it didn't help South Vietnam then the whole of South East Asia would fall to communism like a line of dominoes; the same USA that used the infamous Gulf of Tonkin incident as justification for entering the war in Vietnam. Robert McNamara, the Secretary of Defence at the time, later admitted that the Gulf of Tonkin incident never happened! Over a million people died as a direct result of that deception and the domino effect turned out to be just more scaremongering.

In my youth I read Private Eye, it was the only publication that printed the news as it was, not as the powerful newspaper barons wanted you to see it. The media moguls have always had politicians jumping through hoops in the hope of extracting concessions and exchanging favours. It is only with the Freedom of Information Act that we can now see just how many visits to 10 Downing Street some of these moguls made. Some were there so often perhaps they should have claimed a second home allowance.

The last of these Pillars of the Establishment that has traditionally been held in the highest esteem, is the church. If people wish to hold certain spiritual or religious beliefs then that is their right, but why they should be considered wise or moral as a consequence is not so obvious. Take the story of Abraham, common to Christians, Jews and Muslims alike, who acting on God's command, tied up his son Isaac and was about to kill him as proof of his faith when an angel appeared in the nick of time and told him to stop. Well, I don't know how well that would stand up in a court of law but if I were Isaac I'd have been more than a little concerned about my father's mental health. The story seems about as believable as the Scientologists conviction that humans are immortal aliens called Thetans, extraterrestrial creatures trapped on planet Earth in a physical body. The fact that the founder of Scientology was a science fiction writer may have some bearing on that notion. So people will hold whatever spiritual beliefs they choose, despite a paucity of hard evidence to support those beliefs, if indeed there is any. Ultimately, 'faith' is the last resort of those lacking a rational explanation. What they are really saying is, "We know we are right, so believe us!" which was quite a useful argument for early civilisations but most of us need something more convincing nowadays, at least, those who think for themselves do.

It has been said that the only difference between a religion and a cult is the numbers and, on that basis, religious leaders in the past often demanded their say in how the country was run. Now, that is no longer acceptable. In one of the world's most secular societies, where substantially less than 10% of the overall population attend church regularly, by what logic does religion deserve the right to preach to the rest of us?

The old defence of raising the moral standards of society relies on the application of a moral code that is filled with complexities, contradictions, and hypocrisies that were originally designed to support a long outdated status quo. Processes that have led to ongoing scandals such as the abuse of children by priests who were moved to a different parish rather than exposed, defrocked, prosecuted and locked away, don't represent a vote winning contribution to a healthy society. People seem to be gaining a greater awareness of these charades now and with the coming of the internet and social networking they are learning the truth even more widely and rapidly. Events in North Africa and the Middle East are recent examples.

When I first started putting my travels down on paper I found it refreshingly cathartic. It is easy to see why, with my attitude, trouble seemed to follow me around like fresh shit stuck in the tread of my trainers. I thought that as I progressed with the story I would see the errors of my ways and resolve to make amends, but that isn't what happened. In the event, writing served to strengthen my conviction that I had been right to stand up to authority and thereby retain my independence of thought and action, self-respect and credibility amongst those who know me. There is an old Chinese proverb that says to survive in life one should be like bamboo in the wind and bend with it; if you stand up straight you will snap. While this may be entirely true, it only tells half the story. If we all bend over and nobody stands up, then we all get shafted and the world is left to tyrants, shysters, thieves, cheats, liars and their cronies, of whom there is never a shortage.

It is not my intention to paint everybody with the same brush, I have good friends who are exceptionally successful businessmen, others who hold strong religious beliefs, and even members of the police force, but I respect them for who they are and not because they are rich or hold high office. I even believe there are some good politicians out there, and live in hope that one day they may actually be elected. Maybe I'll stand myself: it's about time I came up with another plan!

(Boodarai)

And all I ask is a merry yarn from a laughing fellow-rover, and a quiet sleep and a sweet dream when the long trick's over. John Masefield

18
Among friends

About seven years ago I popped into a pub in town for a pint, the place was quiet but the fellow standing next to me looked vaguely familiar. He showed absolutely no sign of recognising me and I was having trouble putting a name to the face which was not surprising as it had been thirty five years since I had last seen those features, and in those heady days they had hair framing them. It was Barry, and he practically fell off his stool when I introduced myself to him; it was frightening to see how much we had both changed, and how close we came to finishing our drinks and going our separate ways, oblivious of each other's true identity. Needless to say, we punished the rum

Return of the likely lads. Barry (L), Simon & me, Plymouth, 2009.

that night and started to meet regularly for a quiet drink, and over our beers we chatted about old times and wondered what had become of some of the others.

A little research soon put us in touch with Simon, Dick, Charlie, and Moz, and the inevitable reunion that followed was memorable in the extreme, as was my hangover the following day! One thing that came as a bit of a surprise, and which we all agreed on, was how little our personalities had changed despite all the years that had passed. Dick and Moz both live locally and, as Dick has a yacht berthed in Plymouth, a few of us take to the high seas on a regular basis to hone our sailing skills.

One fellow who I had often thought about over the years was Patsy. I hadn't seen him for forty years and he was such a character that I decided to try and trace him. I knew his home town in Ireland and searched the net for phone numbers in his name. Unfortunately, as is often the case in Ireland, the name was so prevalent that there were twenty with the same name and initial in that town, and this was on the off chance that he had actually gone back to live there! I rang the first number that evening and explained that I was trying to trace a fellow by the name of Patsy Kelly; he'd be about 58 years old, ex-Merchant Navy and ex-boxer, and I enquired if he could help me. The reply was instantaneous, "Sure, I think I know the very man, give me your number and I'll tell him you rang!" About an hour later my phone rang, "John, it's Patsy!"

The following summer saw my wife and me in Ireland for one of the best weeks of my life; Patsy took us all round the mountains and lakes as our personal guide. Although he was now a successful businessman he still did some pilotage work in one of the local ports, and he told me he had to take a ship out the following evening so invited me along. The Captain greeted us as we entered the bridge and Patsy promptly introduced me as a fellow pilot over from the UK! As we steamed down the river channel we passed a beauty spot where numerous people were out enjoying the evening and, as tends to be the case, the ship became the focal point for many of them. Patsy wandered over to the ship's whistle and sounded out three short blasts and, as a ship's whistle is designed to be heard at a considerable distance, you can imagine how many heads turned to see what was happening. I couldn't understand why he had sounded the whistle because one short blast signals to other vessels that you are altering course to starboard, two that you are altering course to port, and three that you are going astern. I knew my nautical skills were a bit rusty but I was bloody certain we weren't going backwards! When we got out into the bay we bid our farewells to the Captain and clambered over the ship's side onto the small pilot boat for the ride back. I asked Patsy why he had sounded the three blasts and his reply was typical of him, "Sure, that was just for the tourists, they love all that stuff!" Don't we all?

Setting the fashion, again. Me & Patsy (R), Bluestack Mountains, Donegal, 2010.

Q. How long's a piece of string? A. About double the average.

Pub philosopher.

19
Addendum

It was following yet another washout summer that Kim finally decided to realise her long held dream of visiting Australia. I had run out of excuses and suggested she choose wherever she wanted to go, it was, after all, her holiday. She booked a week in north Queensland and I recalled that my old Australian mate Doug, from Crackers bar, had come from there and I wondered if he had returned. A quick check on the internet revealed that there were half a dozen D. Lowreys in north Queensland, but only one within reasonable driving distance of our destination, so I sent a postcard with the simple message, 'Does the D stand for Doug? If so are you the same Doug who worked in Crackers bar in Soho in 1977? Passing through in a few weeks do you fancy meeting up for a coffee?'....and gave my email address.

It was a shot in the dark and I was not even remotely optimistic of a reply, so it came as some surprise when, a week later, an email popped up and the first line, 'G'day y'ole Bastard' gave me an inkling that I had struck lucky. He was insistent that we not only meet for coffee but stay at his house for the whole week, my pleas that we could not possibly impose on him and that we had already booked accommodation elsewhere fell on deaf ears. I'm glad they did. Kim and I had an amazing week and Doug and his wife, Karen, (a true 'Sheila' as any I've met), were perfect hosts. By the end of the week I was speaking 'strine and swigging Tooheys like a local. Leaving was harder than I imagined and the memories of that holiday will stay with me forever.

On the long flight home I reflected on how lucky I was to

have made so many good friends in my life, how grateful I should be that these friendships had endured over all these years, and what a stroke of good fortune it was to have been finally reunited. Once again, my life seemed to be rosy, my daughter happily married with a lovely family and good career, my eldest son a serving Army Officer and my youngest son nearing the end of an engineering apprenticeship with an excellent company. However, there was one small question at the back of my mind, what had become of the rest of my original college class, and would there be any possibility of a reunion after so long?

Those of us already in contact pooled our limited knowledge of their respective home towns and set to work. In a relatively short space of time we found 'Shoey' enjoying his retirement in Sligo, West Ireland, 'Jimmy' working as a Skipper in Oban, Scotland, Phil in Lincoln, 'Gypo' still sailing the seven seas and resident in Brasil, and 'Des' semi-retired in Glastonbury after a long career catching criminals....now all we needed was a convenient place and date. Plymouth was the preferred option for nostalgic reasons and the date, in view of our ages, was sooner rather than later. Unfortunately it proved impossible to get everyone there but with nine out of the original class of 14, plus 'Moz' who was lucky enough to have been promoted to our ranks during the second stint at college, we shared our memories and relived our youth over the inevitable beer and curry. The whereabouts of 'Bellman' and 'Sparrow' are still unknown. But I understand that 'Smoothy Jack' eventually left the sea and joined the police force.

J23. Plymouth Beerological Society AGM, 2013.